Nlp Techniques

Influence People By Subliminal Persuasion, Speed Reading Analysis and Mind control

(Break Bad Habits, Eliminate Anxiety Using Neurolinguistic Programming)

Frisco Barton

Published By **Tyson Maxwell**

Frisco Barton

All Rights Reserved

Nlp Techniques: Influence People By Subliminal Persuasion, Speed Reading Analysis and Mind control (Break Bad Habits, Eliminate Anxiety Using Neurolinguistic Programming)

ISBN 978-1-77485-874-5

No part of this guidebook shall be reproduced in any form without permission in writing from the publisher except in the case of brief quotations embodied in critical articles or reviews.

Legal & Disclaimer

The information contained in this ebook is not designed to replace or take the place of any form of medicine or professional medical advice. The information in this ebook has been provided for educational & entertainment purposes only.

The information contained in this book has been compiled from sources deemed reliable, and it is accurate to the best of the Author's knowledge; however, the Author cannot guarantee its accuracy and validity and cannot be held liable for any errors or omissions. Changes are periodically made to this book. You must consult your doctor or get professional medical advice before using any of the suggested remedies, techniques, or information in this book.

Upon using the information contained in this book, you agree to hold harmless the Author from and against any damages, costs, and expenses, including any legal fees potentially resulting from the application of any of the information provided by this guide. This disclaimer applies to any damages or injury caused by the use and application, whether directly or indirectly, of any advice or information presented, whether for breach of contract, tort, negligence, personal injury, criminal intent, or under any other cause of action.

You agree to accept all risks of using the information presented inside this book. You need to consult a professional medical practitioner in order to ensure you are both able and healthy enough to participate in this program.

Table of Contents

Chapter 1: Effects Of Manipulation.......... 1

Chapter 2: Key Factors in Dark Psychology 12

Chapter 3: Learning Goals 26

Chapter 4: Nlp And Anchoring 42

Chapter 5: Third Pillar Of Nlp 52

Chapter 6: People Are The Best Strategy To Accomplish Anything......................... 62

Chapter 7: Changing Your Mind Through Reframing 73

Chapter 8: Maps of Nlp. 86

Chapter 9: Areas To Use Neuro-Linguistic Program 99

Chapter 10: Is Nlp Good? Neurolinguistic Programming – A Tool For Good Or Evil 118

Chapter 11: Effective Communication To Get Your Message Across...................... 131

Chapter 12: Fundamental Parts And Center Tideas 148

Chapter 13: Practical Use Of Deception Against Other People 167

Conclusion 183

Chapter 1: Effects Of Manipulation

Manipulation happens when people manipulate our emotions and mental status through their actions. In this way, they can gain a lot of benefits. These are eight main effects. They are as follows

It Can Impact Your Health

Manipulation can negatively impact our health and mental well-being. Many people are subject to manipulation through various forms domestic abuse. This can lead directly to traumatic stress disorder. An increased level of anxiety or stress can result in a disordered emotional state, which can be detrimental to your health. People feel angry, sad, and even sick when they discover that they have been manipulated. The shock of being betrayed reduces one's intellectual capacity and makes it difficult for them to think correctly.

Many people will abuse alcohol to the point of drinking excessive amounts. This is in the hope that they feel better when sober. However it can make things worse by raising the body's sugar level, which can lead, among other things, to diabetes, heart disease, or rheumatism.

This could affect your relationships

Manipulation may have many detrimental effects on our relationship. Manipulation in marriage can cause many problems. One example is when a man claims he is going on a business trip with his wife, but the wife doesn't believe him. This can lead to the man ending up at his girlfriend's place. This is a man manipulating his wife out of trust. The man is now able to take advantage of his trust for his own benefit. This is wrong as the wife might find out and file for a divorce.

It is common for wives to be breadwinners and take advantage of their husband's inability provide for their family. Sometimes the husband might quit to be the head of his household. This is another type of manipulation used in many marriages. Because one of the couple was manipulator, so many relationships have ended today. The manipulator in most cases is the spouse who manipulates the other. This can cause isolation and malice within the home.

Friendship is a case in point. There are many cases where "friends who have benefits" situations. When you are rich, friends will want your friendship in order to benefit from your wealth. In some cases, someone may want to be your best friend in order for you to do their/her bidding. These types of manipulations have caused many friends to lose their friendships and turned them into bitter enemies.

As mentioned in chapter one, this can affect both the parents' and children's relationships. We see parents manipulating children to get what they want. However, we also see children exploiting their parents' emotions to satisfy their own needs and desires. They will do whatever it takes to please their parents, even if this means being dishonest.

It destroies self-esteem

Self-esteem must be a core value of an individual's life. It's essential for our everyday lives as it helps us to overcome larger problems. Imagine someone without self-esteem. It is like losing your determination, motivation, ambition, and drive in life. One of the fastest ways to lose self-esteem is to associate with negative minded individuals. These people will manipulate your thinking and make negative comments. They will manipulate your mind using your circumstances to make you hopeless. When you give in, your self-esteem is affected, which can affect your entire existence.

It Can Affect Your Reality

We all know our reality is formed by our perceptions, beliefs and assumptions. If our perceptions and beliefs can be manipulated, it can cause a negative reaction in our reality. For example, there was a happy and healthy couple. Everything seems to be going smoothly. The husband and his wife were happy. One day, the wife got into a nasty argument with her friend.

The woman may think it is all well, so long as it does not affect her marriage. The friend of her wife starts to react. She doesn't like the fact that her friend is happy and has no other relationship. So, she decides to do something. She finds out the past of her friend to be used against her. She sends pictures to her husband of her friend in strippers. When the husband looks at these pictures, everything changes. Because his husband never knew his wife was once an ex-stripper, the stripper photos affected his reality. A happy, healthy, and successful relationship had become a broken one because his friend wanted to manipulate it. Manipulation may change your thinking, make you take decisions you don't like, and make you become something you don't wish to be.

It causes you to have suicidal thoughts

Manipulation could lead to high levels of frustration. It can even lead to suicidal tendencies. You feel like life is not worth living. You believe you're beyond redemption. This is not your thinking.

It Can Have a Negative Impact on Your Business

There are always people manipulating the business. At work, people believe that everyone has the ability to work hard, and do well at what they do. Why is this so? You can only get a salary rise if you work diligently. However it doesn't mean that hard work is enough to get a better pay check. Our office superiors encourage us to believe that the harder we work the closer we will get promoted. These are just manipulation tricks to keep their employees on their payrolls. Even if your efforts are great, promotion is not possible without recognition from the same superiors. The key word is manipulation.

This holds true even if an auction sale is being conducted. It's all important to have a profitable business. The highest bidders will always be the ones who come out on top. The auctioneer manipulates the minds of the buyers in order to ultimately get the highest bidder.

They are internet-based investment businesses that try to scam people. You can find high yield affiliate programs that offer huge percentages and great returns. If you invest a certain amount, they will make you believe you are a millionaire within minutes. Even though you may refuse, their offers can be hard to resist.

Marketing is now the most manipulative field in business. Customers are being convinced by people who go to extreme lengths to get their products or services. They will even offer a substantial discount if they get what they want. It is impossible for you to become involved in a company where you will not be manipulated.

It can make you commit horrible atrocities

All of the negative things happening today are all due to manipulation. It is manipulation that enables a criminal to enter someone's home and steal. There is no such thing as a thief who wakes up and decides to steal. This happens because of manipulation. It has to do both with spiritual and physical facts. Bad company corrupts good manners. You may end up committing crimes you did not intend, but your group can influence you and make it easier for you. All people want to make quick money and some will go to great lengths to help achieve their goal.

In order to achieve their goals, manipulators may commit atrocities even if they leave people dead. Spiritual facts show that everyone has beliefs, and we keep them. People worship different gods to get protection and blessing, or even a sense that they are serving a purpose.

People can be blinded and controlled by their beliefs. They will do whatever is necessary to protect their sacred religion. They follow all rules and obey every sacred commandment which binds them to the gods. In order to please their gods, they will go as far as to commit so many atrocities. Manipulation can be as extreme as religion.

It forces you into making wrong choices

The reason things don't go as planned is what you have probably discovered. It is not because we don't have the skills or potential to succeed, but because something went wrong and led to a bad outcome. When it comes down to making choices, the mind is a battlefield. There are many things that can influence our choices. These include our parents, grandparents, friends, and spouses. These people have an influence over our decisions. Most of the time, however, it doesn't go the way we wish.

It is because of this that we must learn to make right decisions if our lives are to be successful. A lot of times we are manipulated through people's lifestyles. Imagine that you meet a friend who's wealthy and suddenly find yourself with sleepless nights. Then, you start to plot out ideas and venture into something that doesn't go your way.

One friend might be a great singer. You let someone manipulate your destiny into a bad career choice.

You have the parents who manipulate their kids into making decisions they like. Your child is scientifically inclined. However, you want him a lawyer. He reaches a stage where, even though he does have money, he feels disappointed because his parents are preventing him from living the life he dreams of.

Manipulation methods can be very subtle and yet very clever. We must always be conscious of who we are and what our intentions are.

Chapter 2: Key Factors in Dark Psychology

Experts believe that all the traits mentioned above can be found within people with dark personality types. However, there are three key elements that must exist for someone to be considered Dark Psychology. Psychopathy, manipulation, and narcissism all form the foundation of what is known psychologically as the Dark Triad. The Dark Triad provides the foundation for Dark Psychology research. The trilogy of traits, or the trio of common traits that are displayed by those who excel in Dark Psychology.

This guide will give you a deeper look at these traits and show how they can be manifested in different personality types. We'll also discuss how to protect yourself. Keep reading for more information about the dark side human psychology. You will find it everywhere, even in advertisements and people you meet on the street.

Dark psychology and evolution

All humankind started as survivalists. They were hunter-gatherers, who traveled the land searching for food and warmth for animals. These communities eventually settle in agrocultural settlements. This creates rules, regulations for leaders, and a moral code. As these societies grow and develop, art, music, or religion are created to compensate for the limited life they lead within the boundaries of the society they created.

From these beginnings, land was important as well as properties. The production of goods and chattels requires possession. As time goes on, these settlements turn into villages, cities, or cities. Cities eventually become border-forming nations. As was the instinctive nature of humans since the beginning, survival now refers to the entire community and not an entity.

All of these cultures, however will eventually fade away. Many fall as they develop into empires based on their laws and religions, which then dominate the poor. However, history has taught us that cultures can be destroyed for many reasons. (Ancient Greeks and Romans, Egyptian and American French, German, Japanese and German Empires in Modern World).

All these societies shared one thing: they didn't foresee their demise. While it is difficult for Americans and Europeans to imagine the EEEUR or USA falling apart, the new global powers are unable to see the problem. "Capitalism" is their Achilles heel. Karl Marx was aware of the dangers inherent in capitalism and its eventual collapse. However, he couldn't have imagined how it would consume the modern universe to such an extent that the

21stcentury would be dominated over by oil and gas wars.

The problems are not all due to mismanagement. However, there was an increase in funds and the loss of confidence that average citizens had in the financial systems. These factors led to a rush for money and the inability to repay the debt. People panic, and then they turn to the mode of survival.

Dark psychology of fear

How does the organism's response to a threat perceived psychologically trigger a response? The answer is found in the causes and effects of pain within the human anatomy. What was the equivalent of physical pain and psychological pain? Why is pain so common? With physical pain, it is simple. It is not possible to find motor reflexes that are simple and do not require spinal cord regulation. Why does it cause psychological suffering? It is known as self-regulation in all physiological processes. This means that the brain responds to changes in the body's chemical processes. Presumably some sort of alteration occurs due to emotions. Let's call it pain psychology trigger. Understanding how emotions affect an organism's physical health is crucial. Understanding the complex organization of mentality and nervous system is necessary. It is necessary to understand the complex organization of both nervous system and mentality in order to work as a professional.

You may be afraid of darkness. This could mean that you are experiencing heartburn, flowering woodiness, or throat discomfort. You may sound like someone has stopped breathing. Here, you're not afraid to be in darkness. But, you do fear something that can survive in the dark. It is based solely on the information you have accumulated about it throughout your life. You are afraid of what the devil may do to you. A little boy never fears the darkness until he's seen what might be there. Let's call us anxiety conscious.

These fears, such as fear of an event or circumstance, that make you fearful or anxious, are sometimes called conscious fear. They can occur because you have had a bad experience or lack of knowledge. What type of fear is it? What's the fear? What's the fear? Untrustworthy. It's really embarrassing. Discardment. INACTION. Feeling anxious. Blaming. Illusion. Confusion. Struggle. Stress and fear. You are experiencing difficulty in blossoming. It is difficult to breathe. EUR 100 Euros old sweat. Your body experiences physical and psychological sensations. This is why fear can be associated with certain negative emotions. Because one element causes another, it is caused by the other. It means the same.

Consider implicit fear, which is an unbased fear. What could this be, you ask? This could be fear or confusion, or the fear and terror of the unknown. For starters, children fear sounds and other unknown things. People have been fearful of unexplained phenomena of nature since before the dawn of time. Or were they more concerned with the unknown phenomenon that was already known?

Fear of uncertain possibilities, such fear of imagined harmful events, can be frightening. We can't see how these could be bad things. We consider future adverse events to be the same as those we have seen.

Unknown things are what we fear, and we fear the unknown. Because positive unknown things arouse joy, we're not afraid. We forget all the positive things that we do when we feel anxious. So, anxiety arises when we start to see a fearful future and create a bad image. This implies that uncertainty is a deliberate fear.

Sorry and regret - the trinity of dark psychology

Adaptive living can be described as the three words Guilt (Regret), and Sorry (Sorry). When these terms are used, they increase the chance that all social interactions can succeed. Inadvertence and denial of this social trinity can lead to criminal or deviant behavior with victimization as the modus operandi. One of the strongest, most nuanced and powerful phrases you can use in conversation is "I'm Sorry."

Since the dawning of civilization, this term has been part social and cultural interactions in all languages. An important part of social ties is still "I'm so sorry." The expression "I'm sorry" is an example of how humans can be flawed. While words and actions are temporary, they can also cause permanent psychological scarring that is not easily healed. To understand the meaning and context of "I'm Sorry", the reader will be able to comprehend this powerful sentence. There are many meanings to the word sorry. These can include communication that is sent in social situations. If you look at it from a reductionist perspective, the addition of the identifier, "I am", makes the sentence an apology or expression of regret.

An apology can be defined as an act of regret for causing someone else pain or discomfort. Feeling guilty for one's actions or feeling contrite is what you mean by regret. Both guilt and regret are two emotions that people often find difficult to accept and feel.

Remorse, another important term, is needed to understand the simple phrase "I'm sorry." It's hard to feel guilt for any wrongdoings if you don't have remorse. Remorse refers to a deep sense of remorse and guilt over causing harm to others. Depending upon the amount of harm caused, the severity and extent of guilt can vary. Remorse is a socially acceptable goal.

You can't make a change in your actions without realizing that regret makes it easier to live a happier lifestyle. The human race has been trying to communicate and express guilt since the beginnings of recorded history. The survival of society would not be possible if there was no guilt about wrongdoings. Humans are social animals that thrive and flourish in a diverse society. As part of this evolutionary process, both remorse expression and recourse are encouraged. They are both essential for the survival and growth of all species, homo sapiens.

"I'm Sorry" is often mistaken for honesty. This is despite the essence of guilt and regret. An individual's character and honesty are a barometer of sincerity. The result of expressing guilt can be directly linked to their intent. If honesty becomes suspect, then any attempts to apologize can easily be considered as mistaken sincerity zero.

The past, present, or future actions of someone who is truly remorseful have an effect on their character and integrity. Some are irreparable. Others can be recognized provided that relevant works have been exhibited. Actions taken after a misdeed result in new learning behaviors which lessen the possibility of repeating the same mistake.

A person with alcoholism will not be discussed, changed, nor diverted to explain human fallibility. Even though the alcoholic knows that their drinking is causing pain and distress for others, he/she still continues to drink by using various defense mechanisms including denial, displacement, minimization, and minimization.

Alcoholics are committed to the eventual destruction of their character, dignity, honesty and character by others. They will often drink for years before feeling any guilt or abstaining from alcohol use. This is the path that all humans will follow to adapt successfully. It involves the process of healing, appreciation, sorrow, pain, redemption and reconciliation.

There is little chance of meaningful change if you don't feel guilty or regret for actions others find offensive. There are numerous defensive mechanisms to keep anyone from feeling guilty, regardless of how deep the human mind may be. To be able to say, "I'm sorry," requires a deep inner reservoir known as consciousness. According to some definitions, consciousness is a moral sense that distinguishes right from wrong. This psychological construct can influence the behavior of a person and promote functional behaviour. Awareness includes perception, knowledge, consciousness, and knowledge about oneself. This structure is like a glass full of water. The average person's consciousness reservoir is half to

3/4. As described above, a part of the human condition is fallibility and propensity to participate in non-functionalbehavior(s)-- the less knowledge a individual possesses, the less capable he / she is of victimizing others. The most grave consequence of missing a source or consciousness would be a deviant, rapist or sociopathic mindset. The human experience has one of the most significant words: "I'm sorry." Recognizing, regretting, remorseping, and rehab will forever be a barometer for human adaptability starting from the beginning, and going on to every moment thereafter. Laws, religions or philosophies all have the goal of reducing suffering and managing it.

The goal is very simple and requires only five steps of practice.

* Expect others' offence due to the variable bias experiences.

* No matter if you are innocent of guilty, hurting followed by empathy.

* Verbalize your future commitment not to offend.

* Encourage and facilitate a paradigm shift that re offensive acts.

Never forget, forgive and love one another

Chapter 3: Learning Goals

Effective communication

Communication is the best method to express your feelings. Being a social person, you need to communicate, have fun, and share moments. Because goals are tied to communication, it is important to take action to reach your goal. It is important to communicate with other people, to share knowledge, to share experiences, and to make connections. NLP and communication are discussed here. NLP helps you understand communication. You can also see which aspects of yourself affect communication. For the interlocutor it is important that they adapt to their communication style so that it can achieve its goals. It is important to set a goal for every communication.

Every man is a communicator in his own unique way. Communication involves us having our own internal dialogue. We notice how that communication affects us and how we feel. It is because you are rarely present in communication. But how much do your words actually convey? People depend primarily upon words when communicating. But, the truth is that they often say less than they think. Their nonverbal behavior conveys much more information than words. Words convey very little information. For example, take a job interview. While you may have done all you could to prepare for the interview, it is possible that you give a negative impression. Perhaps the other person, once you had entered into communication, took what she did not want from you verbally and nonverbally. It could have simply been that you were provoked to react in a way that was not successful. NLP allows the management of subconscious information that may be hidden or brought to your attention by external factors. NLP communication teaches that "people love people like they are" and this is true for every one of us. Consider the people you are closest to, those you admire, love, and so on. These are people with the same values you have, who also share something that interests you. However, when you confront people who are not able to have the 'that' thing that you want or don't have the 'that' thing that you need, you won't automatically cultivate sympathy for them. You may have greater success in some conversations than you. NLP techniques allow us to discover common characteristics between us and our interlocutor, regardless of what impression we may have had about them. NLP communication is essential. The non-verbal attitude is another crucial aspect of communication. The non-verbal attitude of people can tell a lot more about them than verbal. The nonverbal attitude of a person is also their energy, so if you are not in sync with your partner, your communication will fail.

NLP offers many techniques for helping you to become more aware of the nonverbal thoughts of others. How many times have you encountered people who behaved in an unanticipated way with you? Those moments were not the right moment to be with someone and it was impossible for you to work together towards a common goal.

3.2 Improve your interpersonal relationship

NLP can help you understand what is happening in various situations and what opportunities there are to connect. It also helps you manage communication and get the most out of others. The real question is how do you establish effective communication with each other? Many believe communication is the easiest thing on the planet and that everyone can communicate. It's not easy to know all the words and phrases of a language but to also know how to send and receive a message, conduct successful conversations, and accomplish a communication goal. Language is only a tool, and how you use it can make a difference in the communication of your message. Here are 5 guidelines that will enable you to communicate effectively with each person. Don't make assumptions based on interpretations. It is the most common mistake made in communication: to draw conclusions based only on their own interpretations. Interpretation refers only to one's subjective experience of a subject. It was based solely on an individual's experiences so far. This means that it cannot be used to draw relevant conclusions. This is why communication errors happen. NLP begins with the assumption of that the behavior and emotions of an interlocutor are the best indicators about how they think or feel. To avoid confusion and to be precise, you must be clear about what you see, hear, and feel. Next, define what that means for you. Don't make unfounded assumptions. Most people assume based on their biases and general opinions. Many people begin with an attitude. This is because he understands that touching other people's belongings is against the law. Some people are more relaxed than others, because they've seen other examples. It is fine for them if you take out a pencil from their purse. It doesn't matter what makes sense for you, it doesn't make sense for someone else. One of NLP Principles is "The map is not the territory." NLP says that a map is a metaphor of a personal view of a world. A territory is a metaphor of the real world. One person may change his map during their lifetime. Sometimes, he alters it to make maps more useful. Sometimes he is in conflict with others because their map looks different from his. You need to be able to see the whole picture and not just your own view. Communicate your expectations clearly. How often have you heard this phrase - We expected something different! It is a problem when expectations are not expressed and defined for each side. You can avoid this by asking precise and clear questions. Asking specific questions will give you concrete information that will prevent conflicts. Ask questions. Sometimes people mistakenly believe that successful communication involves a flow of information through multiple mutual statements. Effective communication requires that you get to know your interlocutor. Instead of trying to impress your interlocutor, you should ask him as many questions and as many questions possible. This will help you get details that are relevant to your interlocutor. So you'll know who you're communicating with and how you can adapt your communication to him in order to better understand you. Here are some questions to ask: What is your goal with this communication? Why is this important? What is the purpose of what you are doing? What effect are you looking for? You must be present during the conversation. You have to have been in the store when the seller forced you to learn about a product that was not of your interest. Some people find this a positive experience, while others find it exhausting. You must be present for long-term relationships, and good communication. Being present in the conversation and actively listening to your interlocutor will enable you to understand his needs and provide him with the information he requires. A story without substance is just that: a story. For successful communication to occur, one must be open to listening to the interlocutor and then follow his lead. The results will not be overlooked.

3.3 Work habits

If you have strong relationships with people you value, your work environment will make you happier. After the difficult work of finding a job and the adapting period necessary to make your workplace comfortable, it's time to organize your obligations and understand the work tasks. You can then modify the system to suit your needs. Being able to take responsibility and know what needs to get done will help you avoid being labeled a "bad worker" and make it easier to avoid doing things that are not necessary. The business world has changed. Increased privatization has made it easier to pay employees out of one's pocket. This has resulted in a more productive worker. Not only is a higher wage, but there are other "luxuries", which allow us to be more efficient, more available, more competent, and most importantly, happier. The point is that everyone can get used to pleasant things very quickly. It's only a matter how much they know about it and what they are willing to do to make it happen. You must meet your obligations as a business owner. This is a fact that is indisputable. Your job is meaningless if you're not performing your duties. Respecting the rules of the company is key to being responsible. The unwritten rules can make all the difference in your career. Relations with the employer as well as the team are crucial. You respect your boss. You must treat your boss with respect.

Never offer to help someone or invoke your friendship to the employer. Your leader should not be criticized in front of your entire team. Don't be afraid to criticize your leader with arguments. You may also want to present it privately if needed. Thank your boss for all the support you've received. Respect for your employers, co-workers and associates is an important quality. You will cause disruption to the work environment and reduce productivity by being prone towards conflict. While gossiping at work may seem innocent at first glance, it can cause problems by rehashing the details and making assumptions about who did what. If gossip is used, it can lead to a loss of trust from others and a decrease in credibility. Accept cooperation. Working in a team requires collaboration from several people. Your business should not be viewed as though it is the only thing that exists. Every member of a team shares the responsibility for teamwork. If you leave work, it is a sign that you have not helped someone. You may be able to transfer your responsibility, which is yours. While everyone has their own job description, we should all help others when necessary, even though their job may not be the same as ours. But, you shouldn't make yourself a "duty-omniscient" or interfere where you aren't. Find a way that you can help others. Listen to the people around you. Sometimes, it's more important to be open and honest about your opinions and positions on a topic than to "keep silent and suffer." People you work with share this need. They should be able and willing to listen. You should be kind to all your coworkers regardless of their rank in the company. Respect their opinions, even if they are different from yours. When there is a conflict between motives and interests, the conflict should be solved by both parties. They must also listen, respect and work together to resolve the problem. If you don't have a real need to criticize another colleague, it is best to do so constructively. For the company, teamwork is essential. A healthy environment and higher productivity are guaranteed by mutual respect. If you find yourself in a conflict situation, it is best to not discuss the matter with everyone. It is best to have it done somewhere private and where there are opportunities to discuss it privately. This will prevent you from creating an uncomfortable situation. Don't try to shift the blame to others. Don't make excuses for what you didn't do right or pass the blame onto others. Be realistic and see things as they are. There is an explanation for every situation and no one asks you to be perfect. But it is important that you are self-critical. This is how you can learn from your mistakes, improve and grow. It is important to not disturb others when they are at work. Unprofessional behavior in an office is also a distraction for others. Talking too loudly, asking endless questions and causing distractions to your colleagues are all bad habits. It is not necessary to work in "sterile", but you should be sensitive to the needs of others. Don't delay. Work hours are set for a reason. You should follow them and show respect for the employer and your colleagues. Everyone gets more sleep if they are sleeping longer than you. Your sleep habits and the amount of rest you receive for the following day are up to you. To be able to continue working until the last hour, you must get to bed at night if possible. Also, it is against the rules to sleep at work. Don't be rude. It is not appropriate to use slurring, vulgarity, swearing, verbal, or physical language at work. Avoid quarrels. You shouldn't bang on the door when you go. If you have a problem, it is best to try to solve it peacefully. Aggression won't help. As cliché as this may sound, it is important to respect the places where smoking is allowed. It should not be negative. You might not like the outcome. You can look at the problem in a different way or seek out help from colleagues. You can't complain and it won't help. Your workplace is the second important thing. Responsibility towards the workplace. It is a wasteful use of resources. It is becoming more popular to purchase mobile phones, cars, as well as everything else you need at work. It is not an asset that you can freely use without being paid for. Trust is not a prerequisite. However, there are some exceptions. Sometimes, it might be possible to access business resources at the top with employer consent if there is an actual reason. Recklessness in consuming alcohol and other psychoactive substances while at work can cause serious problems. It can cause a decline in judgment and motor skills as well as injuries and violent scenes. Immoral and illegal workplace actions are not allowed. Responsibility must be a priority. Dealing with this in any area of your life is unacceptable, especially if it means that someone else may suffer. Hygiene should be taken seriously. Personal hygiene is a responsibility of all employees. All employees should be neat and clean. They must also come to work properly groomed (and shaved when it involves the male members of the team, and discretely make up when it pertains to the female parts), with neat hair and nails. The company will also require that employees adhere to all rules and regulations. As a member of a team, you will likely have colleagues with whom your disagreements are less. The ones who can sometimes cause you to be very annoyed. You are unable to concentrate on your work or be as productive without them. You can learn a few ways to deal effectively with people like them. This does not mean arguing, pulling your hair out or going on vacation. Recognize (good) intent behind such behavior. You may have ever wondered why your colleague behaves in that manner. Perhaps your colleague is trying to get attention or insecure. Sometimes people struggle to communicate their emotions clearly and end up making more mistakes than they make. The person who asks you questions all the time just wants to be friends with you. Another example is the one who grumbles and constantly asks for clarification. It is impossible to know exactly what is happening with your colleagues but you can trust that they are trying to help. Recognizing and accepting it can bring you some calm. You will gain a better understanding of the essence of such behavior. Assess the personality types of people who disagree with you. We all have character traits that make up our personality and are part of who we really are.

Chapter 4: Nlp And Anchoring

NLP anchors make it easy to get into a resourceful, productive state of mind quickly. You can feel happy just by flipping the switch. This section will discuss anchoring and the ways you can create it.

Anchoring, one of the most important tools in neurolinguistic programming, is a tool that can help you increase self-confidence, interest, as well as make yourself feel more relaxed. Anchoring is an easy technique that can transform any negative or unwanted feeling in to something positive and resourceful within a short time. By creating an NLP Anchor, you create an involuntary stimulus response so you can feel whatever you want at any time. NLP's anchoring process allows you to associate an inner reaction with an outside trigger or internal trigger, allowing you to quickly and easily assess your reaction to that stimulus.

Pavlov created a conditioning technique called anchoring. Anchoring might look quite similar to it. Pavlov developed a conditioning technique to induce salivation in dogs when they hear the bell ring. Pavlov believed that the bell ringing meant that dogs were hungry. Pavlov realized that his dogs would start to salivate when he rang the bell. This theory assumes that an external stimulus or cue could elicit a behavioral response. The association formed is spontaneous and not due to choice. The stimulus-response conditioning formula is used by behaviorists to condition subjects' response to a stimulus.

Anchoring is a method of relative conditioning, which includes linking between other emotions and experiences rather than restricting it only to external cues. You can use an example as an anchor to determine how you react when you see a picture. An anchor can be the tone of voice, which is associated with a specific feeling, such confidence or excitement. Anchoring can be used to trigger or establish a connection for yourself. Anchoring helps you become a better person. Anchoring is a tool that allows you to start or restart a mental process. This can be associated with creativity, learning and concentration.

NLP's analogy with an anchor has certain meaning. An anchor helps stabilize a boat, or ship, so it doesn't move around and remains rooted in a place. To keep a ship or boat stable and in a particular spot, an anchor is dropped by its crew. An anchor is a psychological anchor which helps to generate a response in NLP. To extend the analogy of a ship to human psychology, an anchor refers the experience we have within our consciousness. Anchors are a point of reference that helps us find a specific experience. They also help keep our attention there and prevent it wandering off. Think about how it will feel to be confident and capable during stressful meetings when everyone is looking at you or when you have to deal with a problem. This will undoubtedly simplify your daily life.

It's very easy to understand the concept. It is the connection between a stimulus or emotion and an individual. NLP anchors function because NLP anchors can be used to link two events. It works in exactly like Pavlov taught his dogs how to salivate when he rang a bell. NLP anchors are something that most people use unintentionally. A large, shiny yellow M could be used as an anchor to indicate a good, tasty meal. It can signal road rage, mild frustration, or even anger when you drive past a set flashing red lights.

The great thing about anchors is the possibility of anchoring certain triggers to an emotionally positive mood. It allows you to feel positive emotions, such as happiness, joy, and confidence, whenever you choose. You will need to be able use your imagination and have at least ten minutes to spare to enable this reaction. An anchor can last from a few days to a month, depending on the strength of your memories.

It is amazing to have complete control of your mental state. You can change your mind at will by being in control of it. Imagine you are able to feel happy, confident and relaxed at will. Imagine changing the way that you feel. Anchoring is the best option if you are looking to change your feelings. It is possible to react intentionally or unintentionally. You might be tempted to quickly take your hand off of something hot. Or, you might contemplate what you should do. It's obvious that you instantly pull your hands away. This is an unintentional response, which is a part your subconscious mind. When something is anchored, it means that your reaction to such an event will be automatic. You won't have any need to consider what you should do. These associations can be both beneficial and detrimental. It can be a way to recall your childhood memories, such as the delicious food your grandmother makes. You might also find that every time you pass a certain place or an object, you are reminded of something bad.

An anchor can be either positive or negative. We create triggers without realizing it, as we have mentioned. These triggers could be both positive and/or negative. It is important not to let go of any negative triggers. Instead, replace them with positive triggers. Is it possible that you are reminded of a past bad time by passing by a place or wearing a t-shirt? Maybe you were in a bad relationship. The clothing or the place that reminds you of it is a reminder of those bad times. If you spend too much time reclining on the couch, will it cause you to feel depressed? Is it possible to feel the urge for unhealthy snacks when feeling down? This is one example of a negative anchor your mind creates. Positive anchors can be made, and negative ones can be removed. Positive psychology forms the basis for anchoring. The following section will discuss how to set up positive anchors.

Anchoring is an easy technique that allows you create or break associations. To trigger a consistent response it uses different stimuli, including sound, image touch, smell and taste. This is a technique that we all use in our everyday lives, whether we are aware of it or not. In advertising, anchors are often used by brands. They associate their products and services with positive feelings by using pictures of people enjoying happiness, success, or enjoyment. However, this can cause negative associations. It can cause discomfort if the clothing is worn during painful events. If you have had dental surgery and you were wearing a certain shirt, it will remind you of the pain. Your brain has created an association between the shirt and an unpleasant incident. Most anchors are not intentional. However, positive anchors can be created to remind you about something positive.

In all perceptional systems, you can create an Anchor. A variety of anchors can be made: auditory, visual, kinesthetic and olfactory. A visual anchor is a combination of images and words that bring back memories. An auditory Anchor can be a song or a phrase that brings back memories of a specific event. Kinesthetic Anchors can be a hug, a cold breeze, or even a hug. They can also remind you about someone special or a certain place. You can activate your senses of smell by using olfactory or olfactory links. The smell of a perfume, for example, can remind you of someone. Gustatory links trigger your senses of taste. The taste of a certain dish may remind you of your childhood.

Anchoring is a way to get feelings, a mental state, or other resources whenever you like. It allows you to replace an unfavorable feeling with something that's more pleasant. It can help control your emotions. If you are able to control your emotions or reactions, you will be able to have greater control over the events in your life. A happiness anchor can be used to help you feel better if you feel anxious or stressed.

Knowing what an NLP-anchored is, the next step is to learn how you can create them for yourself. It is easy to remember the parameters for creating an anchor. I-TURN stands to represent:

* Intensity

* Timing

* Uniqueness

* Replicability

* Number of times

These are the parameters that will make a strong anchor. Intensity is the first parameter that memory must meet in order to function as an anchor. If you want your anchor to be powerful, the memory you use must be strong. Simply choose a strong, reliable memory, tweak the submodalities (a subset modalities - visual, auditory and olfactory - to make it more intense.

Chapter 5: Third Pillar Of Nlp

Sensory Acuity

"Sensory acuity" is the third pillar of NLP. It is the ability have clear sensory channels (Visual, Sound, Touch and Smell) to gather as much data possible.

We knew this already: our language gives meaning to our experiences. This is what determines the quality and quantity of our behaviors. Better meanings create better behavior. NLP is the art and science of giving more meaning to our experiences.

Better meaning allows us to have more control over our lives. For better meaning to be given it is necessary to have as much data externally as possible.

We are more likely to take data from the Territory, or the External World, and to generalize and deform it. In this process, we might not pay attention (delete) to other data that could help us to understand the experience. Although our preconceived notions wouldn't help us gather data, they may prove wrong. We are unable to have more "Aha!" moments. Wisdom is the ability of having more "Aha" moments.

This exercise will help us gain a better understanding of the concept. I will assume that you are reading this text from your favorite chair, in your favourite room. Simply put the book down on your lap and close your eyes. You can now see the room in your mind's eyes. As much as you can, see as much as possible and dive into details as deep and as detailed as you can.

The color of the table, window and door as well the curtains' design and colors. See how much data you can get.

Now, close your eyes. Take a look around the room. Compare what your open eyes see to the images in your mind's eyes when you were closed. They are not the same. Most likely, they would not be identical. However, there may be many differences in how we remember what we saw and what actually happened.

You can also look around with your open eyes and find anything new that you haven't seen before. It could be small items that you are not familiar with, like how they are laid on the table or on the shelf.

Look for new things. You'll find many things you don't even know about. Just look at your hands and find the details you missed. It could be the smallest wrinkles, color pixilation and veins standing out or the small scars. Or maybe it might just be the hairs standing out in an odd wavy arrangement.

Similar to what you did before, listen to any noises in the room. I believe that you could identify many sounds from the hum and squeak of an air-conditioner to the dull sound of the television in your hall to the faint babble of voices from your neighborhood, as well as the occasional bark of a pet dog.

Now notice any sensations on the skin you don't remember. The temperature, pressure and pressure of the chair that you're sitting on is exerting on your back. Also, the sensation of this book on the device or book you're reading from, exerts pressure on your fingers. The light rustle on your skin from the clothing you are wearing is also important. You can search for any smells or fragrances that are not obvious in the room. Also notice the taste of the food you are currently eating.

This simple exercise will help you understand how much data is being deleted, all while you're still in your world, between your ears. NLP asks you to be more aware what is happening around you, and with other people.

Milton Erickson was, according to legend, resigned to his bed at the age 17 after he was struck by polio. Lying on the bed, Erickson noticed that his family members were using body language more than he did, and began to pay more attention.

He noticed that his sisters would say "Yes" while their bodies were actually saying "No". He could identify the incongruity between what people verbally said and what their body language meant. These observations are said to have led him to his current career as a clinical hypnotherapist.

NLP's most important belief is that you cannot communicate. This simply refers to the fact that people communicate all the time. A form of communication is presence. Absence is also a form. Silence is another form of communication. Body language and tone can make a big difference in communication.

Mehrabian research indicates that out of three forms of communication, body language, tone, and spoken word, body language is most effective (55%) followed by tone (38%) and finally the spoken word (7%). For your convenience, this communication pie is provided below.

It is believed that mankind has only been speaking one language for 10000 years. The body language, however has been the primary language for humans for thousands upon thousands of year. Because it is more fundamental than spoken language, it has a higher authenticity. It is more difficult to tell lies using body language. When compared to lying using the spoken word.

Therefore, if our senses are able to detect patterns in the body language, and its congruence with spoken words, then we may be able to more accurately understand people and identify them.

Even though the words themselves are pleasant, the tonality or the manner in which they are spoken speaks volumes about the speaker's mind. A genuine welcome smile can be much more pleasant than a formal "Welcome!" word with a Sarcastic tone.

There are many things that can be observed about someone, depending on how they express themselves. Here are a few of them:

-Body position (forward lean, backward lean, left lean, right lean or erect)

-Facial expressions. (Many colors and micro muscle movements).

-Hand gestures

-Breathing Rate

-Speaking speed

-Eye movements

-Pupil size

- Pauses

- Specific words

Sensory acuity could be described as the ability to perceive all these cues and adjust to the speaker's mental state. NLP is not like conventional bodylanguage literature. It does not ask you to associate specific meanings to particular bodylanguage cues. This is called mindreading in NLP. It would not be very useful.

NLP asks us instead to calibrate... that is, observe the sensory-based happenings and trace them. Associating those changes with the mind state of the speaker will help you understand and determine the dynamics of their mind state changes.

Calibration can be described as the ability to detect and measure changes relative a standard. The standard could be the client's physiology at session's beginning. Calibration involves comparing two sets of nonverbal signals and identifying their differences. It assists us in identifying and observing unconscious nonverbal responses as well as the associated mind states.

"When in doubt always question ..."" is an NLP Mantra. It is important to not assume the mind of another person, but ask them about it.

On a deeper level, having a sensory acuity over ourselves could prove very helpful. How do you carry your body the most? What's my favorite facial expression How fast can I talk? What is my rate of speaking up when asked about this matter? What are my dominant gestures? What impact do my gestures, tones and words have on those around?

These are some questions we can ask ourselves to improve our awareness of ourselves. This could help you to manage your behavior and can make you more emotionally intelligent.

Also, it's important to assess your progress using sensory acuity. Any progress can easily be measured by key parameters. It could be as simple as

-Number

-Number and type of clients acquired

-Number

-Number

These parameters can be used to help us stay on track and move towards our goal. It also allows us to correct course immediately, so that our goal is not diverted for extended periods.

This shows that the execution of the NLP third pillar "Sensory Cuity" is very important.

Chapter 6: People Are The Best Strategy To Accomplish Anything

The meaning:

Sometimes it's easy to envy someone who has achieved something you had always wanted.

You may have experienced this before. But, what if you were told that anyone who achieved something can do it for you?

Sometimes you feel like you don't deserve success.

If someone has achieved something, then you should believe that anyone can have it.

Here's what you should do

The truth is that you can achieve anything if your efforts are put in. Don't compare your success to others, but instead create your own success.

It is possible to achieve anything by having the ability to create or achieve the results you desire.

This was some advice I offered to help you achieve your goals. However, this advice could prove to be detrimental to you, especially if it is based on your ego.

It's easy to forget the blessings you have and to always aim to accomplish what others want. This presupposition can lead to you chasing goals that don't suit you and will make you unhappy. For example, you might not want to become a doctor simply because your cousin or parents are doctors. It is important to think carefully about the goals that you wish to reach in your life.

Benefits you'll get:

You will stop comparing you to others. Comparison will only make you miserable.

Your life will be free from envy. You will be able to achieve your own success. Not the success you see in others.

All activities should encourage personal growth

The meaning:

You will find many useless methods that they teach in selfhelp or other areas. While you might be familiar with fake gurus who say they can solve any problem, in reality, they just want you to buy their products.

You should make every effort to improve your personal development. This book should be promoting your personal growth. It is worthless if it does not (if you don't do something about it),

This is the action you should take

Every process you learn or practice must promote personal growth. It is essential that you know all the information that you learn so that you can apply it to your life.

Pay attention to what you are taught and how you receive advice. If you get it from the wrong person, it will ruin your life.

Learning is a passion. You will enjoy learning by taking courses, reading books, and getting mentors. Get involved. If you don't act, all information is meaningless.

Consider your habits and what you are doing with your life. Are they helping you grow personally? If so, it's high time you make a change.

As you probably know, what you do everyday is what defines you. Your habits and how you live your life now will determine who you will be in the future. Let me know what you do everyday so I can predict how you will behave.

To give an example, if your habit is to read in the current, you will be educated. Good health and good fitness are guaranteed if you practice regular exercise.

Benefits you'll get:

Choose the processes that foster personal growth to become a person who understands what he does every day. This is how you become wise.

If you choose the right methods, you can make your life more manageable. You will master your life. It all depends on the process you choose.

This will allow you to be the best possible version of yourself. If you choose to have positive habits that promote personal development, you will be able to become the best version possible of yourself.

Calibrate Only on Your Behavior

The meaning:

This presupposition is not the same as number 2 "People do not behave like this".

We, as humans, can learn about the behavior of a person.

Sometimes, you may be able to get some promises from people. But when it comes time for commitment, you will not see anything. You should not believe their words but rather their actions.

Here's what you should do

The best way to understand someone is to not listen to his every word, but to learn about him and see how he behaves. Don't judge him by his actions, but try to "analyze him" by his behavior.

It doesn't necessarily mean you shouldn't judge people by what they do.

If you're a coach or mentor, ask your clients "what are your struggles, why are you feeling so bad and "what are you doing, what are you doing ..."

Benefits you'll get:

You will be able understand and judge people better than you judge them.

You can't be a naive person because you cannot judge people by what or how they look.

All of these traits will allow you to be strong and confident, and wise because you can judge and understand others.

You'll be a great supporter because you know exactly what is missing in someone else's life. Because of course, it's impossible to trust someone speaking about himself 100%.

People Are Not Broken:

The meaning:

You are NOT BROKEN I repeat, YOU ARE NOT BROKEN. I am aware that you don't agree with me. In fact, this presupposition conflicts with a lot of philosophy and psychology schools. Of course, anyone can disagree if you tell him you aren't broken. You will be receptive to professional therapists.

To be truthful, I'm not here trying to convince anyone of anything. The map is not the territory as we saw in our first presupposition. This means that my beliefs are not yours. You should now focus on the next few words and decide if this presupposition suits you. You are free to think as you please.

While you may not be broken, we are implying that the majority your pain and suffering in life is only created by your thoughts. Your pain is only 90% real. We will see that you live a happy life, and that it is better than the lives of many others around you. You can see the difference between people who have no place to call home and those who are unable to afford food.

Your problem is that you constantly look at other people who have more than yourself. This causes you to compare yourself with others and creates the belief that you are not good enough because you don't possess what they have. Funny thing is, people who don't own what you do have have to feel less broken than those who have it.

If you believe you are damaged, you can just be a victim to your own self-deprecating beliefs.

Here's what you should do

Stop being a victim. You must stop complaining about things that you do not find worth complaining about. Guess what, the people you complain to are also "broken", and they can't help you in most instances. I don't think you should hide your feelings or your pain. But you must stop complaining about issues and situations that are not part of your daily life.

Sometimes complaining or having a victim mentality is just going to make your life worse. This is because it feeds the belief that you are not good enough and keeps you from moving forward.

It is important to stop comparing your blessings and those of others. This will ruin your happiness and make you feel desperate. Instead, be grateful no matter what size it may be. Be grateful for everything.

Is your ego your enemy? Your ego can make you believe that you are broken or that you require more help than any other person on the planet. You may also believe you need to have more stuff and live better lives than your friends. When you don't, you feel unhappy and broken. Don't let your ego get in the way of your friends and family.

Instead of complaining about the lack of something, try achieving it. You can make your goals a goal. Your actions determine where and what you will have. However, your goals should not be driven solely by your ego. Don't let your parents dictate your goals. Your goals should be yours, not theirs.

Sometimes it's possible to manage serious mental health issues without professional help. The good news is you can get through this. You aren't broken, but you need help to move on in your life.

Benefits you'll get:

If you can see that you're not broken, it will make you a happier person and increase your happiness. This will help you stop complaining and adopt a victim mentality.

A small ego is not what you need. It will destroy your happiness. Although your ego can make you feel good about oneself, it is only temporary. Your ego will make you miserable long-term.

You will also be able see clearly what you are doing in your mind. You will be able understand others better which can lead to other benefits such as being able to ask for help when needed. You will recognize when you truly are "broken" so that you can seek help.

Chapter 7: Changing Your Mind Through Reframing

Now that you have an understanding of NLP, you are likely to be interested in learning how to use NLP techniques to enhance your communication. A warm surprise awaits you. NLP is not something you have to learn. You are familiar with the process and have already used it numerous times. The reason you may not know about it is because it happens in your unconscious.

Though reframing is an unconscious process it does not mean that everyone can get the best result. Are you a person who has tried to overcome a bad habit but failed? Here's your solution. Reframing can be a key element in NLP. It will help you to win.

NLP Reframing

Take a wall that hangs in your house and replace its frame with something else. Look at it from a distance. Is it similar to what you see? Most times, the answer will not be "Yes." You just used "reframing," to create a brand new image from an already existing one.

NLP's "reframe" is the process of changing the meaning of an event or communication by altering its context. It could refer to the context, content and setting of the event, as well as the person's perception. Reframe can be described as a new way of looking at a situation.

Reframing: The NLP approach presumes that every behavior is a function and consequence of a positive intention. Reframing means to separate a negative behavior and its positive intentions. This allows the person responsible for the behavior to be replaced with better behavior according the same positive intentions.

This explanation is much more straightforward than all the technical details.

Are you a boss? You likely felt hurt and angry about being excluded and may have tried to resign. A different way to look at the situation is to accept constructive criticism, and then use it as an opportunity to improve.

This is a positive attitude that aims to improve your life and get past being marginalized by your boss. Negative behavior includes getting angry and being hurt, then sending in your resignation. A more positive attitude is to be open to criticism and work on yourself. Both positive and negative behaviors can be used to frame the situation. Reframing means choosing a positive outcome instead of a negative one when you assess the situation.

Do you now get the idea of reframing as a part and parcel of everyday life? We use it often to interpret what happens around us. Every time we try to make sense of events in life, we choose one view over all the possibilities. This ultimately leads to our lives and decisions. The process of reframing allows one to avoid collateral damage.

Types Of Reframing - Content & Context

Content Reframe – Have you ever been in a situation that you were disturbed by a power cut during a presentation but your colleague managed calmly to continue speaking under the exact same conditions? Your meaning of the situation, namely that your presentation is doomed because of power failure, is different from your colleague's. How you focus on an event will determine the outcome of your behavior. The power outage itself is not meaningful. If you perceive power failure as a nuisance, then you will be more annoyed. Instead, you can see power failure as a chance to recollect and you'll be more prepared to resume your presentation once the power comes back.

This is called content reframing. It's the act of seeking a new meaning in a situation.

Context Reframe - This means to give the same behavior another meaning. Different contexts can give behavior different meanings. If you have a tendency to use different colors ink for your notes during self-study, this can be helpful to highlight different topics. But it is not useful when you are writing an exam paper with time constraints.

Reframing the original behavior does not change its meaning. This is done by relocating the behavior to a different place, in a new situation, and changing its meaning. Can you picture a situation when a negative behavior, such as procrastination or procrastination has a positive effect on your life? You can apply it to overeating. By avoiding overeating, you can delay eating your dessert after a meal.

Six Steps to Reframe Your Life

Recognizing the sequences of events that result in a change in perception is important, even though it may not be conscious, will allow you to reframe consciously.

You can reframing in six stages. An example has been provided to illustrate the six stages.

Step 1: Recognize the behavior or negative feeling that needs to be changed.

As an example, you may find yourself cramming for your assignment all night because you procrastinate to the last day. This is the negative behavior that needs to be changed.

Step 2 Communication - Determine the cause of the unfavorable behavior in your unconscious and attempt to communicate with it (let's call your unconscious "the mediator", for convenience). If you have a request, you might be able to listen to the sensory signals, such as mental images, sound and tactile effects. Recognize the mediator's responsiveness, it will always help to be on positive terms.

You are the one responsible for inefficient task management. Tap your organizer for a moment and ask it if you'd like to change its action. A response might come in the form a mental acknowledgment, or a slight shift in sensations. We pay close attention!

Step 3: Positive Intent- To isolate the positive intent of the mediator. You can do this to identify the positive and negative intent, and attempt to change the unwanted behavior while keeping the intention. The positive intention can also serve a second purpose. It helps the mediator have an optimistic view of himself, increasing self-efficacy and being more open to change.

Your intention is to complete the task within the deadline. This will give you enough time to examine it. Even if your behavior caused you to delay your workload, this still represents a positive intention. Accepting this fact will help ensure that you start your journey to positive change with an optimistic outlook. It won't be accompanied by shame or regret.

Step 4: Ideas and Solutions - open the door of creativity to come up with new solutions. Be grateful once more for the creativity that you offer.

You can consider alternative approaches to your task completion strategy, such as:

* Develop a target system in which the task is broken down into sub-components that you can achieve each day.

* Set up a reinforcement system where you will reward yourself with an incentive if you reach a certain target.

* Use reminders on a mobile phone or pop ups on your computer screen to alert yourself.

Step 5: Evaluation- Show the alternatives to your mediator for evaluation. Talk to the mediator and attempt to find a solution. Not forcing the mediator to make a decision is not an option. This may result in temporary relief that could lead to internalization. Continue to step 4. Try to come up with more acceptable alternatives.

Ask yourself whether you are open to trying a new approach next time you receive an assignment. If your unconscious tells your subconscious that the alternatives you are considering are too complicated or unrealistic, then come up with more options that will be easier. Don't guilt trip your unconscious into submitting to your conscious demands.

Step 6: Objections, Internalization - If all is well and the mediator accepts your alternatives, it will replace the negative behavior in the environment with a positive outcome. Changes in your perceptions and behavior might have an impact on the environment. This may need to be addressed.

Sticking to the target system could affect your time management skills. This means that you will need to schedule time every day for the task. This will require compromises as well as prioritization for your other chores.

The last step is to look for ways you can internalize the change so that you do not have to reframe the situation for the future.

When do you use Reframing

Practically every day. Reframing is useful when you feel upset, angry, hurtful, out of control, sad, or otherwise insecure. You will likely find it hard to dwell on a negative situation for too long if you're a healthy person. Reframing your situation will give you the relief and comfort you desire. Consider asking yourself, "What other meaning could this be?" Instead of "Why me?" Your predicament will be clarified if you use the "Why me?" approach.

Is Reframing a Type of Denial

The common misconception that reframing means you are trying to make a positive situation better by sugarcoating it is not true. Are you trying to deflect reality by giving yourself an artificial reason? Reframing isn't denial. The content reframing process reveals that an event is not assigned a particular meaning and can assume whatever connotation it has. Reframing means accepting reality and choosing a different way to see it. If you can see a setback as an opportunity to improve your life, rather than being victim to it, then you have reframing. It is liberating to think differently.

Some useful tips on reframing

* Practice positive self-talk. You can learn to value yourself and your efforts. Positive thoughts are better than negative thoughts.

* Now ask yourself: "Is there a better way to see this situation?"

* Ask yourself to find three additional explanations for this event. A challenge to your team is the best way to increase your morale.

Self Help: Think about possible reframes for the following situations

* A group of friends has planned an excursion. But it pours heavy on the day.

* An intimate relationship ends

* You are fired from you job

* You fail a test

Chapter 8: Maps of Nlp.

It is the way you understand the world that determines everything. It affects our interactions with the world. It is responsible for our emotions, our behavior, and our tendencies. Because of the mental maps, it controls everything. These mental maps can be extremely powerful. To control them is to basically take control of the mind.

In this chapter, we will discuss this in depth. We will examine the different ways that you can control other people's minds, and your own. We will look at the fact we are all controlled by the mental maps that guide our lives. What are our mental maps? They will help us to see how we can fit into reality. These are our navigators. They show us how we can accomplish so many things in our lives. They give us a sense of the world around and allow us to comprehend it all without having to worry about what the effort might be. It is not necessary to stop to look at a serpent and then consider whether it might be dangerous. After you have considered whether or not the snake could be dangerous, it's possible that you will have already been bit. It's better to be proactive and not wait until the last minute to consider survival.

T

We will be looking at how he used generalizations throughout the chapter. We will examine how these generalizations, and those perceptions, become the maps we can use for navigation in the world. Then we will look at the relation between mental maps made using NLP and those created by you. As you read this chapter, you'll be guided through how people see the world. You will be able to see the patterns of how people interact with each other and also better understand how you interact and interact with the rest of the world.

O

Reality: Your Perceptions

The world is constantly bombarded with sensory data. Your view of reality is different depending on where you are, and what your position is. It doesn't really matter where you are or who it is. Your view of the world will be different than someone else's. This is because your perception of the world is constantly changing. You will find that understanding the reasons behind your worldview is easier if you remember this. All you need to do is learn to read the maps.

Y

Our senses take in data all the time. Although you may not realize it, your senses are constantly taking in data. The unconscious mind (which we'll be talking about in the next chapter) is extremely perceptive. This means that it is constantly aware of everything within your sensory perception. Even though you may not be paying attention to or focusing on the subject, your unconscious mind is aware of it. Imagine this: If you've ever been in a conversation with someone and then suddenly saw a ball flying at them, did you duck? Even though you may not have noticed the ball in your conscious mind, your unconscious mind was alert enough to make you duck.

T

These perceptions can, however, quickly transcend sensory recognition and become pattern recognition. Imagine that you are in an intimate relationship with someone. Your perceptions can quickly change according to how your relationship develops. You may notice that your partner sighs loudly when you make mistakes. His shoulders slump and he looks disappointed or annoyed every time you say something that is not in his favor. Even though you might not be aware, your unconscious mind is watching. The unconscious mind is aware that you have this issue. Your partner does the same thing every day. It then associates making a mistake with being a disappointment. It may not be something that is in your conscious mind, and you may not even notice it, but every time you make an error, you tell yourself that others have been disappointed. You think you have made a mistake, and you need to correct it.

Y

These automatic thoughts form our perceptions of reality. It is built upon how others respond when you do certain actions. It pays attention how you interact with other people in certain situations. It recognizes the fact that you navigate the world through your experience over time. This allows it to help you understand how to behave.

E

Everything that you have ever experienced influences the perceptions you have of reality. Every aspect of your life, from the experiences you had growing up to the struggles you have experienced throughout your life, has an impact on how you see the world. They all influence how you perceive the world. It is possible to think of spiders as frightening if you have seen them before. This could mean that you were bitten. Or, it could be that someone else was panicking over a snake. This could be because you have learned something about spiders that makes them scary. Your perception of reality is what makes you fear spiders.

Y

You will form opinions about everything you see. Even though people do not like it, we are very likely to make our own assessments about the world. As these evaluations are made, they are applied to every situation. Pretty quickly, you will have your own mental images of the world. This is a crucial point to remember. You must be able acknowledge them. Acknowledging what is happening will allow you to see the way you interact the world. This can help you better understand the way you navigate the globe. These judgments and perceptions are the basis of how you interact with reality. They will guide you. They all help you to build your mental maps.

T

Mind and Mental Mapping

What is also known as mental mapping is when you combine all your perceptions of reality to create a map. Mental mapping is the process of creating the path you want to follow in the world. It creates the way you can better understand the world and navigate everything you discover within it.

W

It comes down to this: these maps dictate how you interact and perceive the world. These maps will guide you in how to interact with the world. If you use mental maps to guide you through the world, it will be easy to see how you are actually following your programming.

R

Be aware that the mental mappings you create are your internal processes that affect your behavior. These mental maps will determine how you interact. These maps will determine how your gut reacts to the world around them. These perceptions are formed over time. These perceptions are what make you and the world around you unique. If you want healthy behaviors, you need to be able ensure that your mental map is healthy.

U

Last but not least, your unconscious mind also contains the mental map you have. They exist under your perceptions, but they are there for you to use and understand. You need to be able and willing to take a step back and observe the world around you. Only then can you begin to see how you think and change the way you think.

NLP and Mental Maps

The mental maps you have created are something that can be easily influenced. It doesn't matter whether you are trying to influence other people's mental maps, or your own, the fundamental idea applies: You are always somewhere within your mental map. Your perceptions of reality will always shape the world in which you live. To expect or assert otherwise would be foolish. This means you need to accept that the world in which you live, or at least the perception of, it, is not the same as the world in which your neighbor lives. Your upbringing and life experiences will affect your perceptions of things. This is a big problem when trying to understand other people.

T

His mental health can also be affected by other factors. What can you do to correct the negative images or beliefs that were created in an effort to prevent them from being negatively influenced? How can you ensure you or someone you know is capable of creating a healthy mind map.

U

Finally, you can learn to influence those mental maps. You can learn how to change the way you interact with the outside world. This will allow you to control how you interact. There are several ways you can influence others' mental maps.

F

If you pay attention, you can expand those mental mappings. If you find that the mental maps are too narrowly constructed, you can begin to widen them so that they can be used to assist those who are most in need. The mental map you have created can be extended. It's your map that you need to expand upon. Look at the way you view the world around. Examine the interactions that you have. If you look closely at how you perceive the world around, you will likely see the problems. Doing this, and gradually expanding your mental maps until you see the world through a narrower lens, will help you to recognize that the problems you are having can be overcome.

S

It is possible to use a mindmap to help you organize your thoughts. Instead of trying expand the mental maps, you'll take the time and reflect on the current situation. If you are able to identify the situation and address it within your mental map, then you can begin to make changes. This mental map can be influenced if you can take control of the events around you. The ability to exert influence on yourself and others can help you redirect your mental map. If you are able to better influence the metal maps, you can begin to understand the factors that will make you a successful person.

F

Although they are not designed to affect the mind, NLP can be used to help you. NLP can help you gain flexibility in your mindset and allow you to think more clearly.

W

If you really think about it, you can determine if your mental mapping is constructive by reflecting on others' mental maps and self-reflection. Let's face it, it's easy to reflect on whether one's view of the world will bring joy or enjoyment to one's daily life. Are you going to find happiness with it? Is it satisfying? Are you really enjoying your life? Or are you feeling trapped or stuck in conflict all the time?

W

An inefficient mental map can make it difficult for you to succeed, and the other person may also struggle. With a healthy, balanced attitude it is difficult to live happily and enjoy your life. This is not because you or your mistakes are wrong, but because you have a biased worldview. It is important to understand how to reorient your worldview to make you feel at ease in your own skin and the environment you live in.

Chapter 9: Areas To Use Neuro-Linguistic Program

Neuro-linguistic Programming can be very useful in establishing a direction where communication is crucial for one's development and efficiency. NLP's services are more extensive if you have a strong communication and development skills. NLP is flexible and can be used to address the

following areas: These are:

Business life and economy

NLP can be used to build trust and communication in your business. This is how NLP was established for many years. It is part of the company's standard for trainers. Neuro-linguistic program is a supportive skill that helps to see the world from different perspectives, to create better relationships with people, cultivate the relationship between the boss, supervisor and colleagues, and overcome cultural barriers in multinational businesses.

Corporate culture today includes training in rhetorical and representation skills. Many managers and executives rely on the creativity and innovation of neuro-linguistic programing to help them develop their company, determine future strategies, strengthen team building, and ensure quality management. NLP is being increasingly used to teach sales personnel.

Discover your potential

NLP is used by many people for the purpose of overcoming unwanted limitations. You can overcome fears, bad habits, and restrictive thinking. A new structure is created that is more dynamic. NLP gives you a lot of communication options so that you can make better decisions to create the life you want. There are many ways to make NLP work for you. These are possibilities that were once beyond your reach.

NLP used in psychotherapy counseling

The use of neuro-linguistic program has been a common practice in psychotherapists and other psychosocial institutions as well as counseling centers. It's based on highly-talented, innovative therapists. They also support clients who have made lasting and positive change.

Patterns of speech, creativity and behaviour were never in the inner circle conscious perception. With some luck, the therapists came into closer contact with this. It was possible to identify patterns and provide information through precise analysis.

Many people worldwide have also learned the skill of neuro-linguistic programing. When it comes to personal transformation, the different processes offer a wide range of options and sustainability. NLP is used frequently to treat phobias. This opens up the client's individuality. Always, there is an examination of the inner as well as outer circumstances. This helps to integrate the change in the context values, social connections, and other areas of life.

NLP coaching

NLP has been a key tool in coaching, in particular in the business, industry and administration. Neuro-linguistic program is used as a consulting form to assist individuals, teams, and groups with their difficulties. They plan and implement new ways of doing things and offer support in developing their capabilities. This is how goals can be clearly defined and strategies developed.

In the health sector

NLP is an ideal tool for nurses, doctors and other health care professionals. Healthcare provision is rapidly changing. NLP can be used to improve nursing and medical knowledge. Patients demand that health care workers have high levels of social skills and flexibility. This includes the ability and willingness to work with others, as well as the ability and capacity to manage a business. This is because the healing process can be directly related to patients' beliefs and communication. The healing process is affected by the social environment as well as the design of hospitals and doctor's practices.

Neuro-linguistic Programming is a way to give doctors and nurses the ability to have harmonious relationships with patients and staff. Also, it helps them communicate clearly and concisely. This contributes to health promotion. As neuro-linguistic programs have become more popular in recent years, it has gained importance as NLP increasingly focuses on how one's personal health can be improved and maintained, how stress can decrease, how one can activate their body's self-healing capabilities, and what methods are available to connect manifested beliefs, attitudes, or assumptions with health.

This question answers the question, "What is the difference among people who recover from an illness and others who don't?" This field is continually evolving.

Creativity

NLP coaching and training can be beneficial for authors, musicians, writers, songwriters, songwriters, singers and other creative professionals. They know how to unlock the creative mind. Robert Dilts of the USA created the Disney strategy. This strategy is strong in demonstrating how to free blockage and how stimulate and release creativity.

Instruction and training

NLP also aims for a conscious understanding and integration of new knowledge with existing knowledge. This provides teachers, trainers and parents with interesting strategies to assist students in achieving higher performance.

Neurolinguistic programming is incorporated into teaching methods and leadership. NLP is a great tool for counselors, pastors and educators who work with groups.

Parental education

NLP makes it possible to improve communication between parents, children and teachers. You can communicate clearly with your child so that he or she can understand what you are saying and how to respond. You can increase the likelihood that your child will not do something if you tell it. Fearful behavior can be caused by a loud, commanding voice or a fearful tone. The following message is a good example: "Don't worry! It can cause the child to worry more. If you tell your child to be careful and to remember that everything is fine, then you've achieved what you were looking for.

Your child's behavior in the world and its environment can be viewed and understood by you. Show your child how to visualize his state in order for him to be confident in school and within the existing educational system. This will help you to recognize and deal with the child's situation, even if you don't like it. Parents are only human!

Neuro-linguistic programming provides parents with a way to give their children clear, effective communication. They also provide the necessary tools for their children's learning and development of self-esteem.

Reframing - Cleverness or denial

It can sometimes be helpful to take a different view of situations and events. It is especially helpful when there is no movement. You can use psychology to reframe your situation, which is also used by neuro-linguistic programmers. NLP also uses the effect reinterpretation to make things clearer and bring you closer to the solution. Reframing not only helps with crises, but it also makes life easier and gives you more joy. But what exactly is reframing?

Reframing: Reinterpreting with a method: one definition

Frame is a technique used in neurolinguistic programing and family therapy. Reframing happens every day, sometimes completely unconsciously. These events are interpreted using certain expectations, thought patterns, assignments. They give them a specific framework which can change depending on how the day is perceived. This allows you to interpret the situation in either a positive, or negative way.

Negative interpretations mean that there is an unacceptable restriction on certain aspects. It can make it difficult to live with these negative interpretations in the long-term. To change something, anyone who wants to can resort to positive thinking. Theoretically this is called neuro-linguistic program or reframing. This means that things are not viewed as negative, but rather positive. But how does Reframing really work? It is simple. It is easy to give an event or situation a new meaning by linking it with another context. Here are some examples.

There are several factors that affect how you approach a situation. These include the shape and attitude of your mind, both positive or not. Both can be reflected in reframing. Reframe a glass of water that is half full. It's the famous question "Is half full or half empty?" The same picture will emerge if you examine it objectively. Perspective is a key factor in many aspects. These are practical examples taken from professional life.

These examples will undoubtedly raise the question about whether reframing can be a denial or creative way of dealing with reality. Critics call this self-deception as it is used to make the negative things pleasant. However, those who focus only on the negatives are not understanding what reframing and neurolinguistic programming means. It isn't about suppressing unwanted feelings or emotions and quickly putting on rose colored glasses to create a happy zone. Positive sensations and thinking are just as valid. Negative thoughts, feelings, and situations such as anger, grief, also have a place in the world.

The key to reframing is finding the right kind of mediocrity. For example, Intveen says:

Everyone knows that bad information can have an effect on your mind and make it difficult for you to focus. In English, this is called a blow in the forehead. This moment, the brain is overloaded with stress hormones. They make it hard to think.

This deficit is not well-known by many. The obvious is overlooked, namely those things that immediately grab your attention. It is no longer possible to find small successes or beautiful things in the past. They are now lost to time.

Again, the event that your dream job is cancelled is averted: self-deception means telling yourself you don't want this job. By doing this, you can put aside all of your negative emotions. At the same time, you are preventing yourself from looking critically at yourself. It must have been for objective reasons that you were not able to find the job of your dreams.

When reframing is used, an experienced situation takes on new dimensions. If you want to succeed, your question must start with "What is it for?" But it is often asked first: "Why?"

Intveen offers a great explanation of why asking "Why" is not helpful. Her assumption is that the gaze is focused on the problem. The mind is like a hamster wheel. It can't stop nor escape from the problem. There aren't any satisfactory answers. These answers might come from the company. You cannot guarantee an honest answer.

On the contrary, if you ask the question "what for", then you look for the context and new possibilities.

* How can I make use of the experience gained?

* What is the point in refusing to do something?

* What good is it to stay with your familiar company?

Reframing makes it possible to take action again.

The phrase "Who knows what this is good at?" has been repeated many times. This little sentence does not imply resignation. Instead, it shows that the person is able to look at situations and events with a lot of humor. It is normal to experience setbacks. How you handle crises can be a crucial factor for your success. This is why it is essential to develop resilience. You will find it easier to manage future problems if you start earlier.

A key aspect of this is to improve your self-esteem and be able to achieve your goals. It is possible to reframe things to make them work again. Karin Intveen believes reframes expand your thinking and takes you out if uncertainty and anger. It also helps you regain some mobility.

"What is it useful for?" Can be used at any time and anywhere. This question may sound questionable considering the many crises we are currently facing. The reality is, however, more real. While it's easy to see the loss of employment and lack of income in this manner, it's also possible to look at the background from a different angle.

* There is an opportunity to reposition your self and do something new. To realize yourself.

* It's your time to look for a job with more money, better colleagues, and flexible work hours.

* Now I have time to care for other people and things dear to my heart.

Reframing questions can lead to funny and ironic responses that make you giggle when you examine them closer. These questions can be funny or ironic, and will spark new ideas. The most important thing is to always be on the go mentally.

You have no limit to the ideas and thoughts that you can create with reframing. This allows you to combine situations and problems with humor, humor, questions, music, and even music. You can recall the rumbling sound of the early hours and imagine Donald Duck grumbling incomprehensibly and turning red from anger. Reframing can be a huge benefit as it allows for relaxation of the entire body. It's much more enjoyable to live and it is easier to be goal-oriented when solving problems. If you think about the problem only in one way: a fixed, rigid approach to solving it.

Neuro-linguistic Programming and Changing Mindset

You may be familiar with the feeling of being overwhelmed by certain situations. Maybe now is the best time to start thinking about how you can reprogramme and change your outlook.

Your beliefs are shaped by past experiences and memories that you have forgotten, but which still exist in your subconscious. This can still have a tremendous effect on your life today. Unfortunately, this can sometimes get in the path of your potential and hinder your ability to develop it further. Neuro-linguistic programming combined with the right mindset can help you overcome such obstacles. But what exactly is Mindset? It is possible to translate and interpret this English word in many different ways. This is an example of how you can interpret it:

Your attitude and your way of thinking about a particular topic will have a significant impact on how you feel, and even how you act. There is a mutual connection that is formed by the experiences you have had. You don't have to be negative about yourself or think negatively. You will also benefit from the positive experiences you have in certain areas.

Maybe you had to present a presentation at school. The school class was resentful because of this. You can still feel the effects of this experience today, when you have to give a presentation. This belief has made it so that you avoid speaking or taking a stand on any particular topic.

If you'd had different experiences in the past, it wouldn't be hard for you to speak today. The positive experiences of the past have helped you become self-confident. You are confident in your abilities and you can make the most of them. Your mindset is like a filter. It determines the environment around you based on what you have done and explores your options. But, it is possible that negative experiences can lead to bad speaking skills. Are you judging your attitude from a past experience and avoiding situations that could lead to you becoming more negative? You may see people who seem to excel in every aspect of life, no matter what the circumstance. You were already born with amazing talent. Stop! Stop! This ability may have been acquired first, and you have done the necessary training.

Carol Dweck, a psychologist who works mainly with motivation, developed an intriguing theory. These two mindset types are based on this assumption. On one side, you have the Fixed Mindset that is rigid and rigid. On the opposite, there is a Growth Mindset that is flexible and dynamic.

Fixed Mindset individuals believe that certain abilities are inherent and therefore are considered talent. They are often blamed for failing to perform at a task because they lack talent or aptitude. Growth Mindset people believe that any task can be achieved if one is committed and has the ability to persevere. This mindset leads to less stress and more success.

Chapter 10: Is Nlp Good? Neurolinguistic Programming – A Tool For Good Or Evil

NLP was also known as neurolinguistic program. This connotation is often reserved for magicians, salesmen and legislators. NLP can be difficult to define. It's also hard to determine what hypnosis is. But if you can see yourself asking these same questions while you hear and see your own responses, you can understand the idea of words building images in our brains. NLP could also be described as having a better understanding of how communication actually works. Richard Bandler's phrase, NLP is focused upon behavior analysis, is an excellent example of this. While positive action results in successful outcomes in a specific context are the norm, LP has evolved to include additional elements and strategies that go beyond beliefs and attitudes.

What's the NLP Mind-Control?

There is no regulation on the NLP consciousness. NLP can be described as a study in communication and influence. Connecting to psychology's new insights and methods, we can develop powerful strategies to control our minds and influence others. It can guide certain patterns of thinking and behavior, but it is not possible for all people. This is especially true if they are invoked and used simple hypnotic terms.

This means anyone who can use these skills for the benefit of others (and the betterment of the world) has a responsibility.

Today's advertisements are so numerous that it is difficult to target a specific section of the population. Scott Adam's Book Win Bigly exposes that Donald Trump (and I believe Boris Johnson) are using simple hypnotic techniques in order to manipulate the electorate.

This is not meant to suggest they are either good or bad representatives. But it does imply that they use specific tactics (which are not based upon evidence or facts) in order to manipulate their electorate.

Is NLP really working for people?

NLP is working with people. All communication is based upon the principle of creating an internal representation from words that conveys information and leads to action or response. When I ask the question, NLP usually means using NLP strategies on other people to get your way. NLP can help to make the audience more desirable or more aversive, but it does not alter an informed communicator's thinking.

NLP does have a Star Wars / Jedi appeal because it was developed by people who wanted to be powerful and could use "NLP mindcontrol techniques However, power is not necessarily a bad thing. To achieve goals and live a meaningful life, one must have personal power. It is important to distinguish between motivating and persuading people to do what is best for them and making them do things that aren't beneficial. NLP can be used to improve your personal and professional life. You will be respected if you create a solid foundation. You will have a happier and more fulfilled life.

NLP, also known as Neuro-Linguistic programming, is one the most widely used forms of mindcontrol in the world. It is used by everyone - from lawmakers to TV professionals to advertising callers. Here are ten things you can do to make sure no one uses it on your.

1. You should be very cautious about people trying to imitate your body language

If you're speaking to someone who might have NLP skills and they appear to be exactly the same height as you, or mirroring your leg movements, then you should check by moving around and seeing if their actions match. Although skilled NLPers can mask these issues better than younger ones, they'll still be able copy the movements of older ones. It's a good idea to call people on their crap.

2. Use your eyes to create random, unpredictable patterns

It is great fun to play with fake NLPers. NLP users are advised to be very attentive to your eyes, particularly during the initial stages. You might believe they are actually involved in what your doing. They are involved, but not because of their thoughts. They monitor your eye movements to find out how you store information and access it. They can tell in a matter of minutes if you're lying or making up things. They can also see what parts of the brain are being used to communicate with you. This can make them so familiar with what you feel that they could almost be calling intuitive intuition. An easy trick to use is to look around and squirt your eyes randomly. This will make it appear natural, but it doesn't have to be a pattern. This is going to make NLP experts completely insane because it will throw off their balance.

3. Never let anyone get near you

This is a common truth and should be obvious. Let's say that you are having an NLP conversation with someone and that you are in a heightened emotional condition. Perhaps you're laughing a lot or getting angry. And the person you're speaking to is touching your hand while you're there. They might touch your hand, for example. What have you just experienced? We grounded your so that they may bring you back to the exact same spot if you want them to. Be going.

4. Pay attention to vague language

Milton Erickson uses NLP's primary technique of using vague language to induce an hypnotic sleep state. Erickson has found that the more abstract a vocabulary is, the more it induces trance. Or, you can use a more specific language to help someone get out of a trance. (Note Obama's use in "Change", a phrase so vague that anyone could learn anything about it.

5. Be aware of the licentious terms

"Stay relaxed." You're welcome test driving the car if that suits you. It is yours to enjoy as much as you like. Erickson was the first to realize this. Professional hypnotists are not going to tell you to do something, such as, "Go into an trance." They will tell clients to "Feel as comfortable as your heart desires."

6. Your gibberish should be kept under control

Nonsensical phrases like "When your exhale this sensation more, you will find you going into the present harmony with the sound quality of your performance more. This gibberish forms the basis of the pace and leading NLP phase. The hypnotist doesn't actually speak, he's just trying to automate internal emotional conditions to push you where you want to go. ALWAYS ask the hypnotist to be more specific or to explain what you're talking. This does two things. One, it stops the whole thing. Two, it forces communication into a specific, specific language. This will eliminate the trance-inducing use, of vague language, that we mentioned in #4.

7. You can read it between your sheets

NLP members are often able to use words that have complex or secret meanings. For example: "Diet, diet, sleep with me are all the most important things. On the surface, this sentence seems like something you'd agree with, especially if it was written immediately. Of course, food and exercise are important. This person just needs to feel well. But what about the more complex message? "Diet and nutrition are the most important things to me. Don't you agree?

"Yeah, you did it accidentally. NLP specialists can be extremely subtle about this.

8. Be on the lookout for your attention

Avoid being in the company of NLP practitioners. This is an opportunity to give an implicit prompt. Here's an example. A NLP user tried asking me to write for his blog free of charge. I looked away and noticed that I wasn't paying attention. He then used the technique described in #7 and talked about how he never needed to pay anything because media outlets would give him free copies of books or albums. He said, "All fair," and began to hiss at the me. "I get everything. For. For. Free. "Obviously, isn't it?

9. Don't ever agree to anything

If you believe you are being led to take a quick decision, then you need to leave. Be patient and wait 24 hours before you make any financial decisions. Don't be tempted to rush to make an emotional decision at the last minute. NLP strategies have been specifically developed for salespeople in order to stimulate innovation impulses. This is a mistake. Use your rational mind to leave.

10. Trust your intuition

The main rule is that if your gut tells or you feel uneasy about someone, then trust it. NLP people often seem suspicious, "off", or like used car salesmen. Fight back or remind them to appreciate you not using NLP techniques while dealing with them.

Three NLP Mind-Control Methods Work Like Heaven

You are interested in NLP strategies for mind control but don't have the right information. You don't have to worry. As I go, I'll give you a brief overview about NLP and share some of my favourite strategies with you.

NLP stands to represent neurolinguistic programming. NLP can be understood from the name itself as it refers to interfacing with one's mind. Richard Bandler (computer scientist and Gestalt therapist) and John Grinder (linguist, therapist) have given their endorsement of the concept.

Bandler & Grinder studied some of the best therapists in the country and were able discover the power and effectiveness of NLP techniques to control thoughts. They were also able to identify areas that could be used for self-development, improving interpersonal relationships, and other useful areas.

You can read on for more information about these strategies!

NLP mind control technique #1: change your physiology

NLP's central principle is to intertwine mind and body. Your perceptions and experiences are reflected in how you walk and move.

Similar to how your body functions, your emotions will also be affected by your walking style.

Your physiology is the first place to start if you want a change in your thought process. To show trust, stand taller, and sit straighter, if that's what you want. Even though you may not feel courageous, smile proudly and be with the men around.

These little changes will quickly make you feel confident about your real life.

NLP mind control strategy #2, word emphasis

It is important that keywords are stressed in conversation. To convince someone to attend an event, you should focus on your command.

Say "Meet at the W Hotel," then pause, and finally say, "Friday night." 7:30." It makes them more likely to agree. Not everyone has to say yes. An automatic advantage is gained by confirming the invitation.

NLP mind control technique #3 - visualization power

If you can see yourself doing what you want, you will be able motivate your mind to follow the path. People are moving to visualization to realize their dreams and goals.

To lose weight, people who wish to do so should use their imagination. We believe that they are at their target weight and maintaining a healthy lifestyle.

NLP mind-control strategies aren't just effective for your own development, they can also be used by others to encourage them to follow your example. Make use of this knowledge and don't hesitate to share it.

Chapter 11: Effective Communication To Get Your Message Across

You have all the information about yourself and other people you have read in the previous chapters. Now it's time to do serious communications work. Neuro-linguistic Programming allows you to learn more about yourself and others. You will become a better communicator, both conscious and subconsciously.

The exchange of information is at the core of communication. You need to be able share the thoughts in your head with others. To do this, you need to make sure your thoughts are clear, well-organized, and clearly stated. Chapter 2 discussed ways to clean your mind from mental clutter. Next segment: We'll go deeper into this concept to help you organize thoughts and find ways to communicate with clarity.

NLP for Better Communications

Use neuro-linguistic program for personal organization is an excellent way to improve communication skills. You can use your visualization skills and create blank spaces for your thoughts to organize them into complete concepts. If you visualize clearing your mind, you will be able to bring in only those ideas that are necessary for communication.

If you start with nothing, you can concentrate on getting rid of your thoughts. While you are visualizing, make sure you only think about the essential things and keep any distractions away.

A table and a filing cupboard are two examples of what you can imagine. You can visualize yourself placing the thoughts that are important to you on the table, and those that you do not require in the filing cabinet. Once you've done this, visualize yourself arranging the thoughts on the table in a way that allows you to communicate your thoughts to others. Take a mental picture to show yourself what your thoughts look like after you've completed that.

Even a mental anchor can help you to recall the images that you have pictured. This could be as simple as memorizing the first line of sentences or creating a rhyme that reminds you of your ideas. When you get to talk or start working on that project, it will be easier to quickly recall how your ideas and thoughts were organized and can easily express them with confidence.

Have you ever been to a debate match at high school? Students learn to think critically and present their thoughts clearly and concisely in a timed situation. Many of the students memorize their talking points. Others use index cards that have small notes or mnemonics to keep them focused as they speak. NLP helps you to organize your thoughts better for communication. Think of NLP as a high school debater.

Talk to People in Their Own Way

We spent a lot on communication styles in Chapters 4, 5 and 6. This included identifying the thoughts and feelings of others and how they communicate with you. If you are comfortable in your communication skills and confident in your ability to read others, then you can be more flexible about how you communicate with them.

You can find your situational voice quite easily. This is something humans do instinctually. It is easier to communicate effectively when you can evaluate a situation and choose the best approach for communicating.

Talking to someone in their own language, tone, and style will show them that you can relate. People feel more comfortable sharing their ideas and are more open for working dialogue when they feel valued and connected. If a coworker uses technical terms in their conversations, you can ask them for clarification or use the terms. This shows your colleague that it is listening and that you can speak or try to understand their language. By asking a question you are giving the other person an opportunity for more information.

When communicating with others, the tone we use is just as important than the words we use. A sunny optimist will speak with you differently than someone who is perpetually pessimist. You can instantly judge how someone responds to your tone, and adjust your voice accordingly. It is a key mark of a good coordinator's ability to read people and adjust accordingly. It is easy to determine the tone of your conversation with a new person if you take the time to listen and look closely during the first few seconds.

To communicate effectively with others through verbal communication, it is important to be mindful of your nonverbal cues. This is especially important for international business and travel situations where cultural differences can affect gestures and acceptable postures. To communicate your tone with someone with whom there is no verbal communication, use facial expressions and gestures. Smile and have an open posture. This shows friendliness and openness will assist you in dealing with situations that may be difficult to understand. Smile is a universal sign of goodwill.

NLP and Persuasion

NLP is a communication tool that allows you to interact with other people. Neuro-linguistic programming has many strengths. One of these is the art and power of persuasion. If you want to make a positive impact on a conversation, this skill will be useful. It can help you in every aspect of your life, from managing unruly kids to landing a big sale at work.

Neuro-linguistic Programming lends itself to persuasive techniques by its very nature.

NLP practice allows you to alter your own thoughts and inner language to effect behaviors. NLP can also be used as a persuasive technique. It can be used to get people to complete tasks, without the need to be asked or commanded. Neuro-linguistic program should not be used for persuasion.

NLP is used to convince people. This means that you use very specific language and techniques in order to get your audience to do what it wants, regardless of how many people they may be. You should not be afraid. This isn't brainwashing. It's using language to influence people's behavior and stimulate their thinking.

It is easy to integrate NLP persuasion within your conversations by asking a loaded query. Instead of asking someone to tell you if they want it, ask them specific questions. This is a classic grandmother's move. Granny might not ask you if a cookie is what you want. Granny can ask you to choose between oatmeal raisin and chocolate chip cookies. Granny created the illusion of choice and convinced you to have a treat. But you didn't have any choice.

NLP persuasion is also useful in everyday life. You should avoid ending sentences with uncertainty. Avoid a lilt in the last sentence. This will make your statement seem more like a question. Instead, your voice should be lower at the conclusion of what you are uttering. This makes your words sound more factual and helps you sound more confident. Try this:

Lilt up, "I'm heading to the campground this Saturday."

Lower down, "I'm going camping this weekend."

Which of these statements had more weight? To make any sentence sound confident or have certainty, you can use this trick.

Another tried and proven NLP persuasion technique is embeded commands. You can either use a statement or ask a question to do this. It's possible to convince someone to take a step back and have another drink at the pub. Try to convince your friend to have another drink by saying "Let's go for it."

An embedded command can be framed with a question. A question can be used to embed the command if you are trying to persuade your child to obey your directions. This will allow your child some control and gives them a sense of choice. If you ask your child, "Do your children want to put your pajamas on first or second?" While they don't have to complete both tasks, they have the option to choose which order.

What if you have a chore you're not keen to do? It's past midnight, it's dark, and your garbage can is full. Do you take the trash out, then put on your shoes and get to work? If you suggest that you will do something, the other person will most likely offer to do the job. You could think of the trash example as:

Direct: Honey, can you get rid of the trash?

- This is not possible to deny.

NLP persuasive: "Oh, honey! I'll take out all the trash if you'd prefer me to."

- This will be often met with a "Don't worry about that, babe. I got it."

One of Neuro-linguistic program's persuasion methods is to use the words '?' and 'but'. This small, yet powerful word can change the tone or meaning of a sentence. You should be careful where you use the words 'and/or' and if you are placing them after a sentence. This is an example:

Negative:

- You've stressed the bad parts of your day.

Positive: "I had no choice but to go to the dentist. But I enjoyed my workout at the gym."

- You put the emphasis upon the good parts of your day.

How you choose your language will impact how people perceive you. Positive things are more important than negative things. This shows that you are positive and optimistic. The word and' works similarly as 'but'. Your position around the 'and' can be more important than your words. Here is an example of 'and'.

Negative: "My day? I had a great work out and had to get to the dentist.

Positive: "My day? Positive: "My dentist had to be seen, and it was a great experience!"

Remember, people will only take in what they hear the last time. Public speakers need to conclude their presentations with strong conclusions. It is why the pastor always puts the lesson at end of his sermon. TV shows also have cliffhanger episodes. The important stuff should be placed last in order to get people to recall and act on what they've just said.

Another neuro-linguistic persuasion technique you might want to use is the one that uses neuro-linguistic programming. It's useful when trying to draw information from another person, not persuade or convince them. Ask them what they would like. It sounds easy, but we mean it: If someone says that they don't have any idea what they want, or where they want dinner to be, there is a good chance they are lying.

These lies don't mean that you are being malicious. Use loaded questions to gather the necessary information. Ask your partner some questions such as "If we had one million dollars, where would we like to go on vacation?" or "If there was a teleporter, what would we like to eat?"

While you and your partner may not be millionaires, nor do you possess a teleporter, because quantum physics isn't far enough advanced yet, it's possible to have an imaginative mind. If your partner tells you that they want to travel to Italy to eat dinner, then find a nice Italian restaurant to make reservations. People will openly tell you what they want if they don't feel limited or restrained. You've convinced your partner.

NLP, persuasion and NLP are both intrinsically linked. This will show you how easy it is to use these persuasion methods at home and at work. Your children will be more willing to listen and less argumentative. And your coworkers will view you as a more confident, strong, and compliant person.

NLP persuasion requires that you also use your nonverbal communication skills. Positive body language is a way to encourage people to open up. Mirroring and matching can also help in building a stronger connection. You've learned a few persuasion tricks and nonverbal cues. Now let's get on with the communication. Next we'll examine NLP's ability to interrupt and reset speech patterns and thoughts of others.

Learning patterns and employing pattern interruption

Interrupting thoughts is a great way to change people's minds. For NLP to work well and better communication, you need to know how to identify patterns. It is possible to use pattern interruption on other people, but it is also possible to use it on your own. Let's examine how it works.

Everyone has experienced a proverbial rut at one point or another. It can lead to negative thinking and disillusionment with your work or household chores. Or, it could become a pattern of repeating the same activities over again until they lose their appeal. How can you get yourself out of a rut? If you are in a similar situation, what can you do?

Answer: You want to disrupt the pattern. This can be done in many ways, depending upon the circumstances. It can be difficult for coworkers to engage in discussions about new projects when they are at work. They're trapped in a cycle, or stuck in the mundane. You can shake them up with vivid language. Be creative and use words you might not hear in the workplace. Ask your coworker for ideas about what might be. Change their routine. They'll start talking to you and be excited about new opportunities.

Look at the reason you feel stuck in a rut in personal life. Are you bored with your routine? You go to the exact same places every week, eating the same food. It is nice to have a community hangout. But it is good for your mental and physical health to mix things up from time to time. Go to a new restaurant or bar and try something new. Find a new activity that you and your friends will enjoy. If you always play darts, go bowling. Thai is the best option for you if your go-to meal is Italian. Find a way you can refresh your social life. You'll make new friends and share new stories with them.

If you are in a mental or emotionally rut, humor and fresh air can help. There are two ways to get outdoors and take a walk. Walking can allow you to think about your problems, but the change of scenery and fresh air can also help you gain a new perspective. Alternatively, you might get so lost in nature that it is hard to remember your problems. This will make your brain more receptive to problem-solving later. You've broken the cycle that has been causing you worry.

The same way humor can be used to get us out of a rut. Ever felt like you were in a terrible mood? At one time or another, we all have experienced such a day. Then, out of the blue, something funny happens and it lifts your spirits. Your bad mood has been interrupted by the funny situation. A little humor can be a great way to lift others out of their funk.

Perhaps you are wondering what pattern interruption means for communication. People, including yourself, can become stuck and it is hard to be open to discussion and new ideas. Communication is best when all parties feel expressive and open to receiving and exchanging information. It is possible to master pattern interrupting and free yourself from being stuck. This will allow you to open new lines of communication with others.

Chapter 12: Fundamental Parts And Center Tideas

NLP can easily be understood by three key segments and their central ideas. These passionate portrayals of experiences can be extended to five faculties as well as language. To put it another way, our abstract cognizant background can be as far as the traditional faculties like vision, taste, tactician, olfaction or gustation. This is so that, when we "see" pictures and hear sounds, "taste" tastes, "feel" materials sensations, think in a few standard languages, and "hear" sounds. Furthermore, these emotional portrayals of experiences have a known structure. NLP is a method of investigating the structure of abstract understanding.

You can portray conduct and grasp it as far as these abstract, sense-based portrayals. The way can be envisioned to include verbal as well non-verbal correspondence, uncouth and maladaptive behavior, and "neurotic" conduct.

Controlling these abstract sense-based perceptions can alter one's behavior and that of others.

Awareness. NLP is based around the idea of cognizance being divided into a conscious segment and an unconcerned segment. The "oblivious personality" is an emotional representation that occurs outside of a person's mindfulness.

Learning. NLP uses an imitative strategy to learn--called displaying--which is said to allow the model to classify or repeat its aptitude in any movement space. A key part of the codification process is the representation of how the tactile/linguistic representations of the abstract understanding are combined during execution of the ability.

Neuro-Linguistic Programming or NLP is a method that aims to bring about change.

First, the neuro or mind segment. Second, the language part. This includes discourse in addition to the five detects (gut sense and instinct), and second, the language part. Richard Bandler in the 1970s was the first to use this term. The Oxford lexicon describes it as a "model of relational correspondence principally concerned about how effective examples of conduct relate to abstract encounters (esp. examples of thought fundamental them" and "an arrangement based on this that aims to instruct individuals and change their examples and enthusiasm in mental and emotional conduct." It is multi-dimensional and requires the use of vital reasoning and understanding of all methods that determine conduct.

NLP was developed by John Grinder and Richard Bandler in the middle of the 1970s. Bandler, Grinder and other researchers were interested in the reasons why some individuals were more efficient than others.

They explored why certain specialists were more productive than others. Bandler held meetings with the three key business personnel to determine their identities and identify the common thread that connected them. The advisors did not give them any information about their conduct. Grinder and Bandler used Grinder's expertise in linguistics to help them make sense out of the example that was inalienable from these advisors. They used language-based modeling to dismantle standards of conduct. This is how NLP was conceptualized.

NLP WORKS ON PRESUPPOSITIONS

We don't have any idea about the true reality. We have our opinions and perceptions of the real world. Our "neurolinguistic" maps are of the real-world, not truth.

The body, the general population, and the entire universe are one in the same. It is fundamental that they interact and have a direct impact on each other. They collaborate and affect one another. They depend in general on rules that search for optimal conditions of parity.

How does it start?

My NLP venture (Neuro-Linguistic Programing) began fifteen years ago. Recently, I had the pleasure of sharing NLP with a brand new group of understudies. Many of these were there just to learn NLP. NLP has been incorporated into many different fields. But, what exactly is NLP today?

NLP (NeuroLinguistic Programing) is a set of devices for self-improvement that examines how we access and store data. It is important to use 'channels,' which can alter reality. This is also true for capacity. Which exercises do we know and which do we ignore? Although it may sound dry and technical, NLP doesn't only deal with realities. However, emotions, sounds or contact can all be used to enhance our understanding of the world. It's not about the mind alone, but the entire body as a whole. NLP is dynamic, fun and exciting.

It isn't unexpectedly a faction' or a large number of convictions that understudies 'need' to acknowledge. NLP courses won't condition your mind.

NLP was first established in California in the 1970s. But, as with all things of thinking its roots go back even further - to Gregory Bateson (1910-1980), and Noam Chmsky (1928-1998).

It began as a study of treatment. Richard Bandler, NLP benefactor, was curious about why some specialists were more convincing than others. He deciphered sessions that were directed by Fritz Perls as well as Virginia Satir (an NLP colleague). John Grinder, an expert in linguistics, helped Bandler to break down these transcripts.

Together, they discovered examples of mediation and organized them into the main NLP apparatus.

The following demonstration was conducted with Milton Erickson. Milton Erickson is a famous subliminal specialist. NLP was then able to assist with the development and recovery of mental faculties and in stupor states. Erickson, who was young and had conquered Polio as an infant, believed that individuals could recover themselves if he pointed them in the correct direction.

NLP's remedial roots have been broadened to include many headings that demonstrate greatness in various fields such as business, politics, and sports. It has allowed itself to become affected by many information assemblages, from robotics through individual-focused treatment.

Robert Dilts (author of NLPU Santa Cruz) is likely to be the most persuasive NLP scholar today. We have a good working relationship. He is an avid reader and has the ability to create amazing change models. Other notable names in the field include Stephen Gilligan (Judith DeLozier), Steve Rae Andreas (Connie Rae Andreas), and Stephen Gilligan (Stephen Gilligan).

NLP is often used to solve everyday problems. NLP is used as a basis in many mentor preparation programs. Many mentors have been drawn to our NLP courses in an effort to improve their understanding of the calling. I'm an ICF-authorized mentor. I have also published books related to the subject. NLP provides the core of our mental display. We are all a result of the universe that instructs.

Mentors shared with us their experience with NLP. NLP is extremely useful from many perspectives, including understanding and utilizing nonverbal correspondence, understanding and deciphering the language themes and in making great compatibility. NLP offers amazing change mediations that mentors and customers can use to help them defeat fears, overcome unhelpful convictions, and manage the relics passionate ensnarement's.

A large number of our customers use Neuro-Linguistic Programming (which we, as a group, have covered up, for different reasons) to increase self-awareness. You can learn more about the methodology by listening to excerpts of an ongoing NLP instruction class.

HOW IS NLP UTILIZED in DEALS?

NLP is also used to facilitate deals. While this has caused some to question its reputation, NLP's business success is an incredible proof that NLP does work. It can't be both incompetent and a cruel personality control instrument at the same moment. I advise our understudies that they use NLP in every day issues. Although deals is the most prominent, many of them need to do some selling. With our business education courses focusing on moral sales, we effectively make it difficult to believe that untrustworthy behavior is possible. Additionally, I feel that understanding how NLP is used to offer us assurance against corrupt advertisers or legislators.

NLP COMPONENTS

Natural Language Processing is (NLP) can also be seen at the crossing point between computational linguistics, computerized thinking, and software engineering. Wikipedia says that this is true. NLP is not about math, Java or C++ but computers that use common language human-created words.

These are just a few examples of NLP. Apple's Siri uses discourse acknowledgment/age, IBM Watson and Google Translate dependent on Machine Interpretation. Google will ask you if you require to interpret if you happen to go to Google. This is NLP. It does indeed investigate content. But, it is not simple to manage the vulnerability of human speech. NLP should be able to extract meaning from the content.

Are you familiar with HAL in Stanley Kubrick's 2001: A Space Odyssey film? HAL could be responsible for data recovery, derivation, and data extraction. In 1967, people enjoyed playing chess, making designs, and engaging in regular conversations. What's more, presently? NLP is visible in Microsoft Cortana. Palantir. Summly. Facebook diagram search. Goodness. NLP is Natural Language Generation (NLG), as well as Natural Language Understanding (NLU). NLU stands for Natural Language Understanding (NLU).

WHAT IS NLP AND HOW DO YOU USE IT?

A GANDER SHOULD BE GIVEN TO SIGNIFICANT PARTS IN NLP.

Element extraction

Element extraction involves dividing a sentence into distinct elements to distinguish and separate them. For example, an individual, association, geologies and occasions. NLP APIs use online information, such Wikipedia or other vaults, in order to coordinate these substances. It can be difficult to coordinate multiple varieties of a particular substance and group them as equals.

Take, for instance, Howard Roark as an element. Roark, Mr. Roark and Howard Roark are all possible varieties for this substance. Calculators should have the ability to group and distinguish all these varieties. There are two major segments in element extraction.

Type of element : Person, place and association, and so on.

Remarkable quality. The importance or centrality (size of a substance) is measured on a scale from 0 - 1. These scores represent the importance of the element in relation to the whole content. Scores higher than 1, for example, indicate a higher priority.

Notice that "Karna," a substance type 'individual, has been dissected using a remarkable quality (0.5/1). This describes the number of events within the content that have a centrality in terms of the whole content.

Let me inform you that Entities/Persons exist in red--Karna as well as Duryodhana. In a similar book, the "world/Hastinapur" will be an area, the "oust/faithfulness" will be another, the "armed force" will be an organization, and the "military campaign" will be the occasion. That's the idea, don't you think?

Syntactic analysis

Language structure refers specifically to the correct requesting words. What structure do the concepts you've created make a "right" sentence. It handles the primary tasks of the sentence's words. After that, you can use a parsing calculator to create a "tree", which will show you the syntactic links between the constituents. This is a good video. Caution! Quality not very good. Separating content into sentences is used in sentence extraction. Tokenization divides the content into tokens (like words and accentuation in natural languages). Standard language API includes syntactic information. Below you will see where the symbols are. This examination covers sentence addition, labelling, labelling, lumping, grammatical aspects, and sentence building.

We'll take part in the Mahabharata portion that was used in the model. In light of the language's general sentence structure, you can see how the words are broken down into their "grammatical elements". (In this model, the root refers to the first action word in a sentence. Karna also has a thing subject relation to "sets aside" and upon is an adverbal one.

Semantic Analysis

The sentence is broken down to understand its linguistic structure and extracted elements are removed. A semantic examination determines the importance of the sentence as an autonomous sentence. The construed meaning might not correspond to the inferred significance. Once the verdict has been parsed, it is possible to comprehend the language structure. The semantic examination will close the sentence's meaning in a sentence that is not bound by a sentence. Induced stress could not be the intended goal of the suggested significaion.

The PC infers that "Karna possessed a crossbow" is a reference to "claims". The PC might interpret "Karna's apple" as "Karna was able to possess an apple" instead of "Karna ate a apple". According to the language rules, the PC might seem "confused". To understand the meaning of the sentence, it will require specific information on the world.

As can be seen from the Syntactic examination image below, the words are interconnected. The PC, for example, recognizes the root action verb and associates that word to the thing "characteristics etc." This part handles lexical semantics. It decides which words are associated to make the sentence meaningful. Lexical semantics is about the importance of segment terms. It can also include word sense disambiguation. "How words combine to frame bigger implications" can be called compositional semantics. It is frequently communicated as a justification. This will make the significance the central focus of a semantic investigation.

Feelings Analysis

After we have completed the semantic and syntactic analysis, we can attempt to understand the slant behind each sentence. Sentiments, feelings, and demeanours will all be included in a supposition. Emotional impressions are not reality. This is also called assessment mining, an asset to web-based life. To decide whether an audit will be positive or negative, you need greatness (degree of enthusiasm for the content) as well as scores (generally speaking feelings about the content). Extremity esteems of original material will be +1, and for harmful material it will be? 1. An archive with an average score of 0.33 and a file size of 3.8 is considered marginally positive, but it will still have some feeling. A long file will likely have high levels of esteem.

It is common to use common sense in the techniques that are associated with brand watches. The diagram that you see below is a real model. It shows the assumptions that media articles should be made for an organization X upon dispatching item Y. The diagram is based on all available public statements. The shocking negative and positive assessments are separately indicated by 1 and 1. The average estimation was determined by extremeness and greatness.

Practical examination

When you ask your editorial manager for a superior sentence structure, she will immediately inquire about the situation. Most often, the complexity of deciphering the meaning of a detached explanation is due to the adaptability inherent in the native language. To get down to earth, investigation uses the setting of expression-- when and why it was said. It manages aims like censure, advises guarantee, demand, etc. What is data or analysis, for instance, when I say "You have been late," The point of talk incorporation is to analyze the announcement corresponding with the preceding articulations, or the entire passage in order to understand its significance. Let's take this example: Chloe needed the announcement. ("It" relies upon Chloe). It is a straightforward investigation that reveals the significance of setting usage not at all similar to semantics. NLP and linguistics view pragmatics from an extraordinary perspective,

Chapter 13: Practical Use Of Deception Against Other People

The ethics of deception in psychology research are a hotly debated topic. Some psychologists think that deceiving participants in research studies is dishonest. But they cannot deny its effectiveness.

Real-world deception is vastly different to what you see in the lab. Real-world deception can be both long-lasting in nature and benefit the liar. This can lead to a qualitative difference in the veracity and method of deception between the lab environment and the real-world.

There are many types deception. Some are for personal gain, others are ideological. Others are designed to harm victims. It is possible to deceive in sports and war.

Deception: Reasons

Researchers have found that there are three major causes of deception in intimate relationships. These include motives that place emphasis on the partner and those that are self-focused.

Agents with partner-focused motives will often use deceitful tactics to protect their partner. To save their partner's relationship, the agent could use deception to keep them safe. This type of deception is often beneficial for the relationship and socially respectful.

This is not as dangerous as some other causes of deception. An agent may keep the subject quiet if they find out something awful that their friend told them about them. Although it is a type deception, it saves the subject's friend and keeps them from feeling horrible for themselves. This type deception is common in relationships, and if discovered it might not cause much damage. Couples would resort to this method of deception in order to protect their partner.

The motive to deceive is not as noble and honorable as the partner-focused motive. Instead of worrying about the subject and how they are doing at the moment, the agent will just be thinking about how they are doing. To protect the agent against criticism, shame, or anger, the agent employs deception. This kind of deception is usually seen as a much more serious offense than that of partner-focused deception. This is because the agent is more concerned with their own self-interest than protecting their partner.

The last motive for deception is to manipulate the relationship. This form of deception is used to prevent any harm from coming to the relationship. It consists of staying clear of relational disturbance and quarrel. This type deception can help or hurt the relationship depending upon the circumstances. This type of deception may be detrimental because it makes things very complicated. It might help the relationship, for example, if you are not open about your feelings about dinner, this could be beneficial. You can also keep it to yourself that you are in an extra-marital partnership.

It does not matter what the motivation for the deception, however. The agent is withholding information that may be important to the subject. If the subject discovers this, distrust in the agent will set-in and they will begin to wonder what other details are being kept from the agent. The deception is not something the subject would be concerned about. They are simply annoyed at not being told certain things. This can lead to a split in their relationship. It is best to maintain truthfulness in the relationship, and not be surrounded by people who use deception in your social circle.

Motives of deception

Deception Techniques

Lying

Many reasons people lie. Truth is, everyone lies about something once per day. This could be the simple white lie (as in the above example) or deeper and more significant lies. You can deceive no matter your motives. Knowing how to lie will allow you to do so without being caught. To be able and confidently lie, you will need the following:

Be aware that lying is just lying. You should practice your lie before you tell it if you want to improve your persuasion abilities. Make sure you do not make it seem rehearsed as you recite it. You can use the tips you have read to prepare. It is essential that you present authenticity and you put the person you are lying about first.

Equivocations

This is an informal fallacy that can be extremely beneficial when trying persuade others. This technique uses ambiguous statements, indirect statements, and contradictory statements to persuade others. When someone cooks dinner for you, they ask if you like it.

Another example would include a feather that is light in weight. This means that it's not dark. The conclusion from this technique is that all feathers must be light in order to be considered dark. This is obviously false. There are many hues of feathers. But the way you stated it leaves no room for argument. You will gain trust and they will believe that feathers can be dark once you have established trust.

Concealments

This is a form of deception that involves not disclosing information that is important or relevant. It may also include concealing important information through specific actions. When you return home, your spouse asks what your day looked like. You tell your spouse that you went work. It was fine. But you don't include the part when you went out with your ex to have lunch. This is not a lie. You're only telling part the truth.

Exaggerations

Although you may exaggerate to make it seem more real, you distort it so that it doesn't always hold true. As an example, let's say you are applying to a job that involves software development. It is asked you if you have experience with software. Because you used Microsoft Word in college, you respond "yes". This is true. It is possible to say that you have tried the software but it does not prove how familiar you are with software.

Understatements

This deception technique involves downplaying and minimising some aspects of the truth. As an example, let's say you went to a party with friends where you drank. You can tell your parents how your Friday night was by telling them that you had a gathering with your closest friends. It is not illegal to lie, as a party can be considered a type of get-together. You are downplaying the reality of what actually occurred.

Be Safe!

Being able to deceive is all about not getting caught. This is because it is important to know who you are trying trick. It is not always possible to know the person you are trying to deceive. The signs of deceit are important to be aware of. Knowing these signs will help you to be aware of them and avoid engaging in deceitful behaviour. These telltale signs are deception:

* You don't make any self-references. If someone is trying deceiving, it is common to simply remove yourself from the situation. Instead of saying they approved a shipment, they might just state that it was authorized. To make your deception more plausible, you'll use "I," and self-reference.

* Using the current tense for events that have occurred in the past. To make sure your message is truthful; you must always use the correct verb tense.

* You answer questions by asking questions. It doesn't matter if your answers are honest or not. Questions can

be seen as deflection, and people will pick this up.

* You are vague. Deceptive people tend to be vague when discussing a particular topic. Giving direct answers is more likely to be believed.

* You must take oaths. These are phrases such as "on me honor" or I swear when making a statement. This is a sign that a person is being deceptive. It is important to get rid of any oaths in your statements. Be direct and concise. These oaths are not intended to increase the veracity, accuracy and truthfulness of your statements.

* Referring to actions. This is what people do when a person doesn't want to have something. This tactic can signal to people that there is something you are hiding. Don't be afraid to speak up, even if it isn't the truth.

* You use euphemisms. This behavior is evident when someone tries to trick you. Instead of admitting to having stolen something, they will say that they borrowed it.

* There is no detail. When trying to deceive someone else, it is essential that you use the right mix of details. If you don't, it will show that you aren't being truthful.

Deception: The components

Unless the agent has been caught deceitful or lying, most subjects won't be aware that these components occurred. These are the parts that can later be discovered if the agent is correctly using deception. Simulating, disguise, or camouflage are three of the main parts of deception.

Camouflage

Camouflage, the key component of deception, is key. Camouflage refers to the stage at which an agent attempts to hide the truth, so that the subject is not aware of the fact. This technique is most commonly used when the agent only partially lies. The subject won't know camouflaging was done until the facts are exposed. The agent will have such a talent in concealing facts that it will not be easy for the subject realize that deception occurred by chance.

Disguise

This is another aspect of deceit. In this instance, the agent attempts to present the impression that they are another person. This happens when the agent hides details about them, such as their real names, where they live, how they earn their living, who they are with and what they do when out. It is not just about changing the clothes someone wears in a play, film, or other media. When the agent uses disguise in deception to fool the agent, they are trying to change their whole personality and appear as someone else.

There are many models that demonstrate the use disguise in deception. The first example is when the agent disguises themselves and pretends to be someone else with the intention of avoiding being recognized. An agent might try to hide their identity in order to gain acceptance among people they don't like, to create a persona that is similar to them, or to achieve their selfish ends. In some cases, disguise may simply mean that the agent hides the true nature and intent of a proposal to conceal an adverse impact. Most often, this disguise can be found in propaganda and political spin.

Disguise may be harmful because it conceals what really is going on. It can cloud the subject's thinking because they don't have enough information to make rational decisions. Although the subject may feel that they are making their own decisions, the agent has provided important information that could impact the subject's decision.

Simulation

This is the final component of deception. Simulation is when the subject is presented false information. Simulating the subject using mimicry, fabrication and distraction are three possible methods.

If an agent mimics another model, they will often give a picture that looks exactly like their own. You may find a plan they like, and instead of giving credit to another person, the agent will tell you that it is all their work. This type can occur regularly via sound-related or visual methods.

Another form of deceit is the use of fabrication. An agent can take something from reality and alter it to make it seem different. They might tell a lie or embellish a real story to make it more interesting or less true. While the core of the story is true, and they may have received a poor test score, it will be altered by the teacher, who might have given them a poor grade intentionally. Although the agent did get a poor score, it was actually because they failed to learn how to read.

Finally, distraction is another method of deception. In this scenario, the agent attempts to get subject to concentrate on other things but not truth. This is often done by offering something that may be more attractive than the truth.

A cheating spouse may think that his wife is starting to suspect him. He might bring home a valuable stone ring to distract them from the subject. Problem with this tactic is that it doesn't last very long. The agent will have to come up with a new trick to distract the subject.

Conclusion

Dark tactics can be used to manipulate you and some people are very aware of their methods. Others, however, may not realize they are using immoral and dark strategies. These people often learned these techniques from their parents when they were young. Others acquired the skills by chance or in their teen years. They used a manipulative tactic, and it worked. They were able to get what they desired. They used strategies to continue to get what they wanted.

It is essential to understand your purpose before you can distinguish between persuasion-based and dark motivation strategies. The purpose of the tactic must be to benefit the other person. It is fine if the goal is to benefit you. But if it is just for your benefit, it could easily lead you into sinister, unsavory acts.

The goal is to have mutually beneficial results or "win-win." But you need to be honest with yourself, and not assume that the other person is in any way benefitting. One example is a salesperson believing that everyone will gain from his product. The customer will also benefit. If a salesperson has this mindset, they can easily resort to using dark tactics to persuade customers to purchase and adopt the mentality that "end justifies what the means." This mentality opens the customer up to all kinds of sales tactics.

To assess our purpose in this interaction, as well as our motivation and persuasion strategies, it is important to ask these questions: What is winning and how can you achieve it?

www.ingramcontent.com/pod-product-compliance
Lightning Source LLC
Chambersburg PA
CBHW071124130526
44590CB00056B/1861